The

Adventures of

Strawberryhead & Gingerbread

The Barking Lot Series ②
Cursive Writing Workbook of Letters!

The Adventures of Strawberryhead & Gingerbread

The Barking Lot Series ②
Cursive Writing Workbook of Letters!

KF Wheatie & KM Wheatie

Strawberryhead &
Gingerbread Press

www.strawberryheadandgingerbread.com

The Adventures of Strawberryhead & Gingerbread
The Barking Lot Series ② Cursive Writing Workbook of Letters!

Published by Strawberryhead and Gingerbread Press
https://www.strawberryheadandgingerbread.com

ISBN: 979-8-9894956-7-2

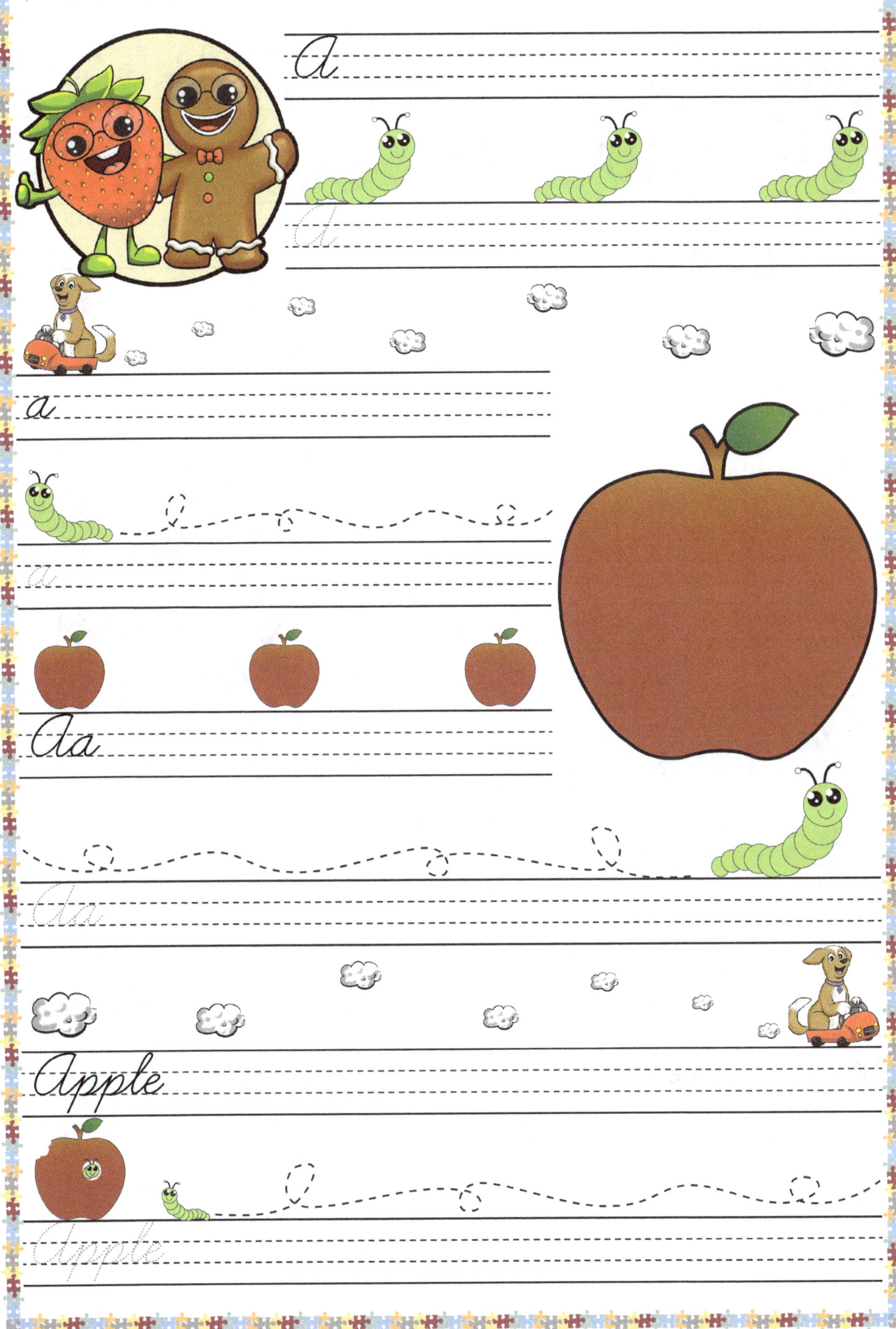
A
a
a
Aa
Apple

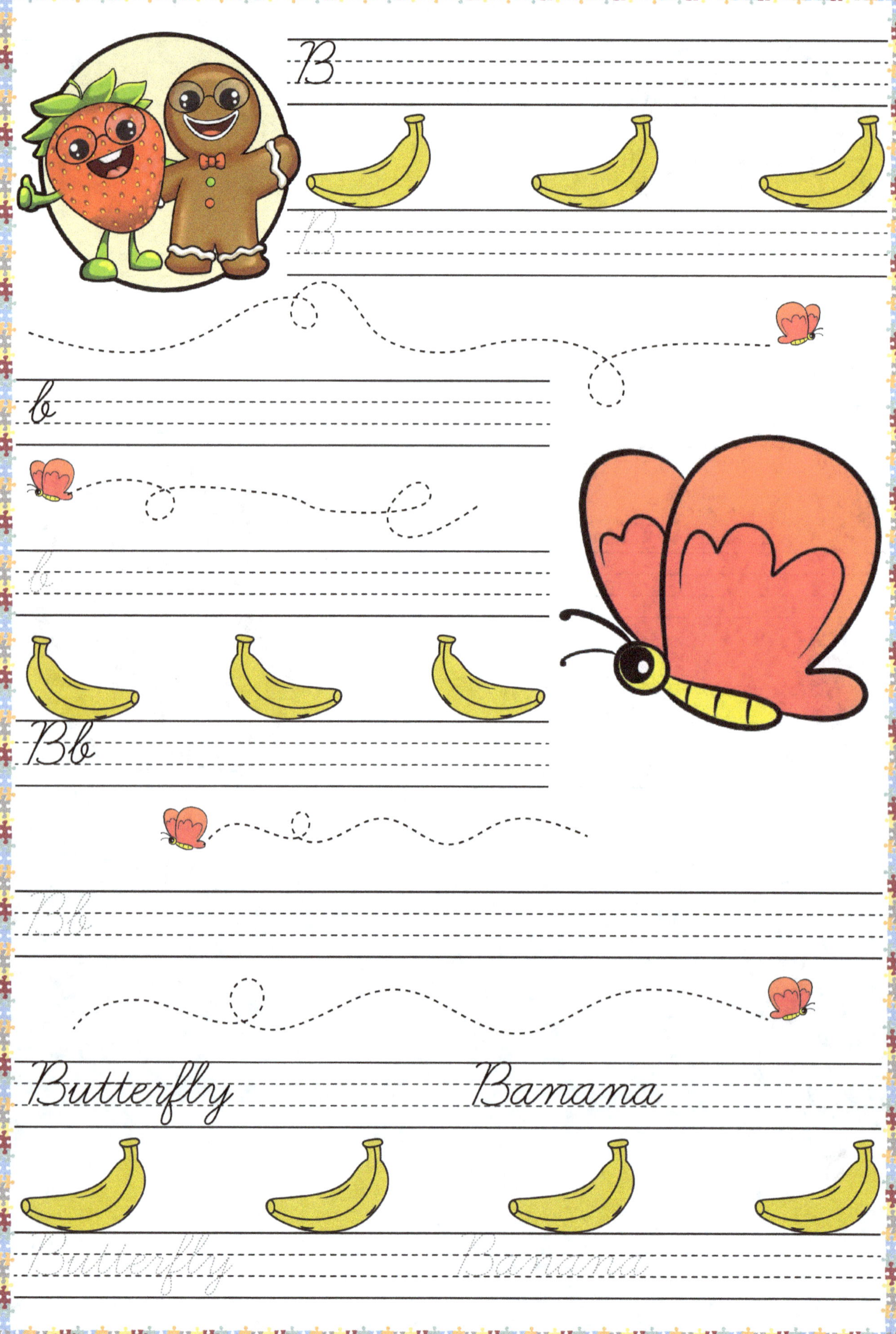

B

B

b

b

Bb

Bb

Butterfly   Banana

Butterfly   Banana

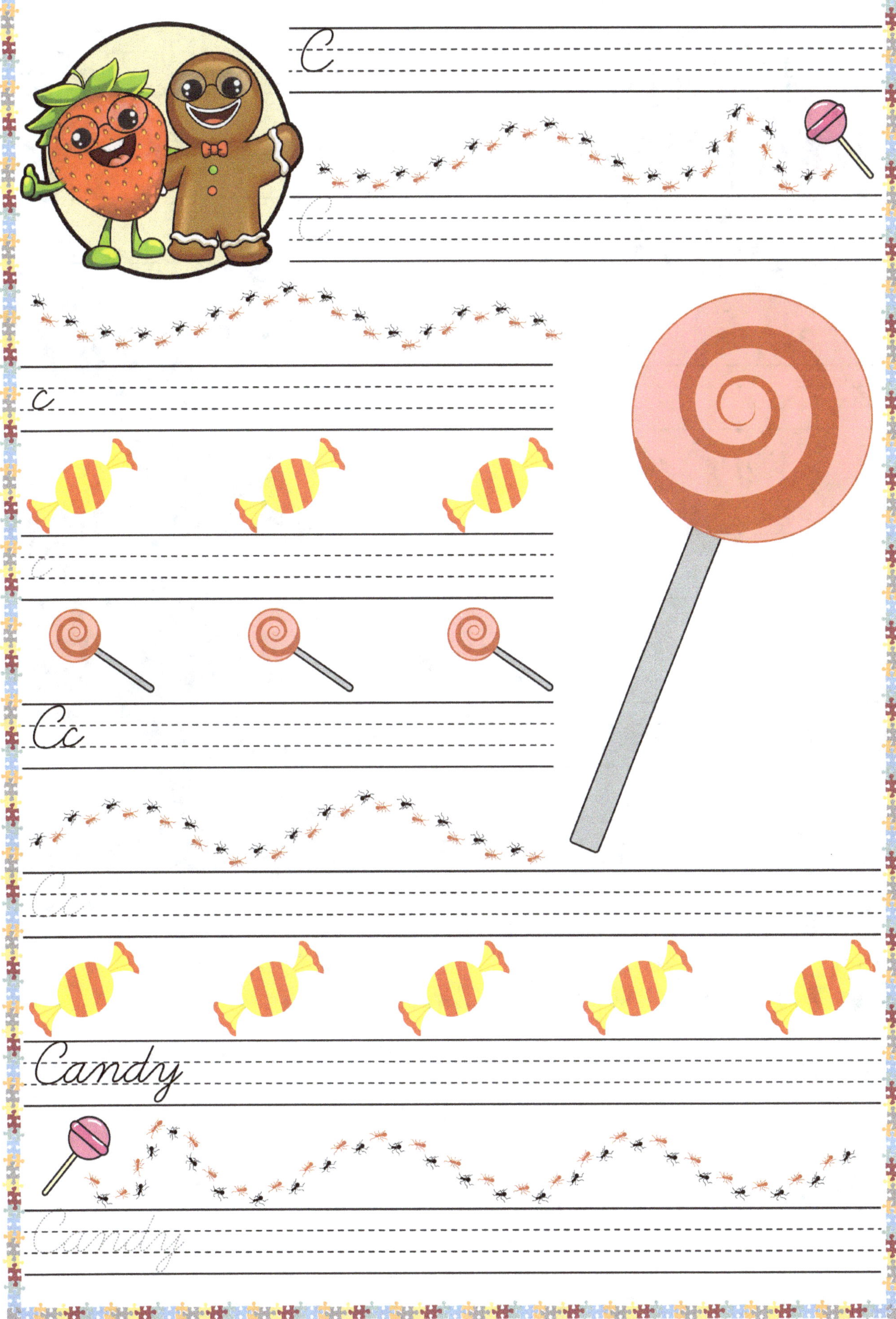

C

c

Cc

Candy

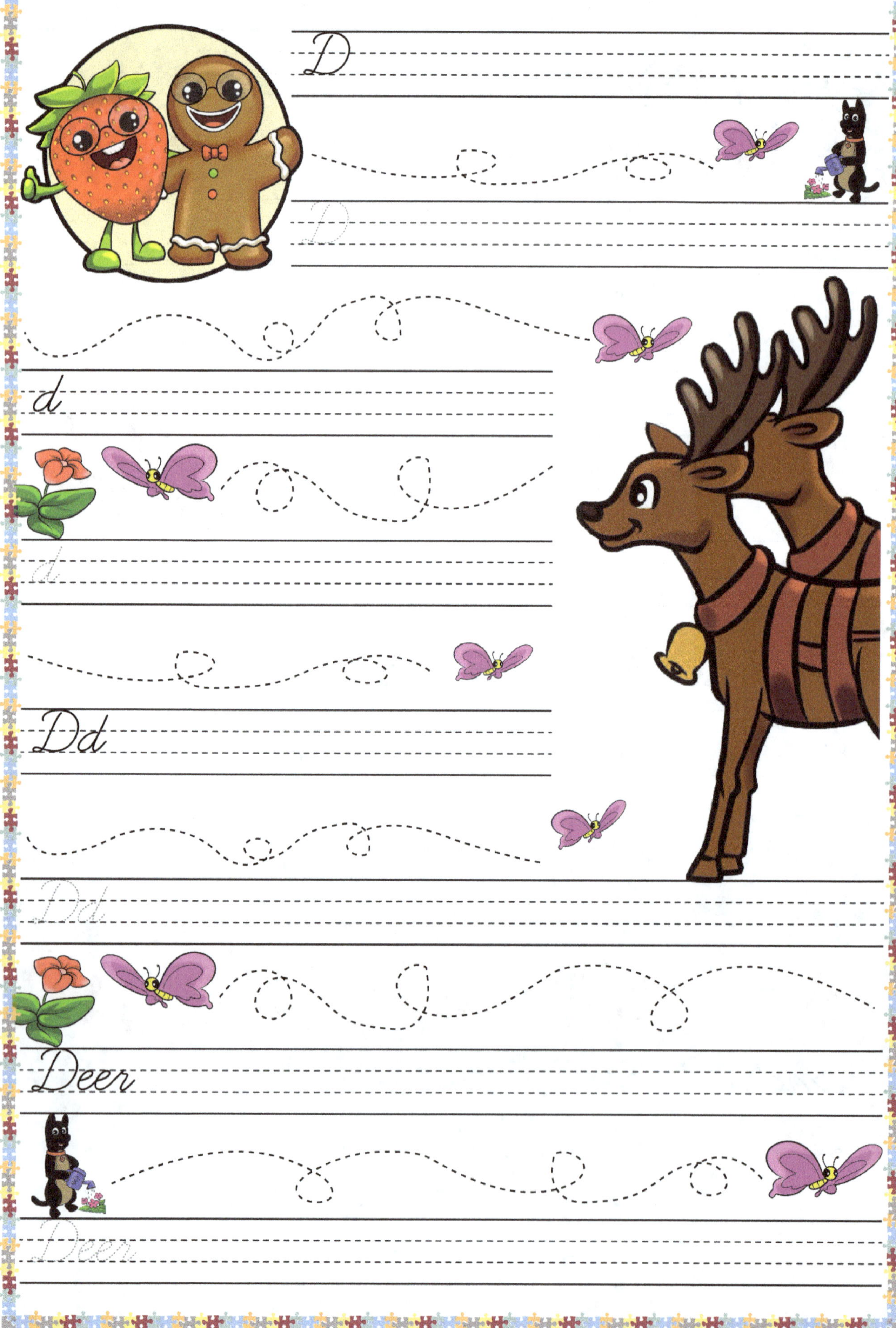

D

D

d

d

Dd

Dd

Deer

Deer

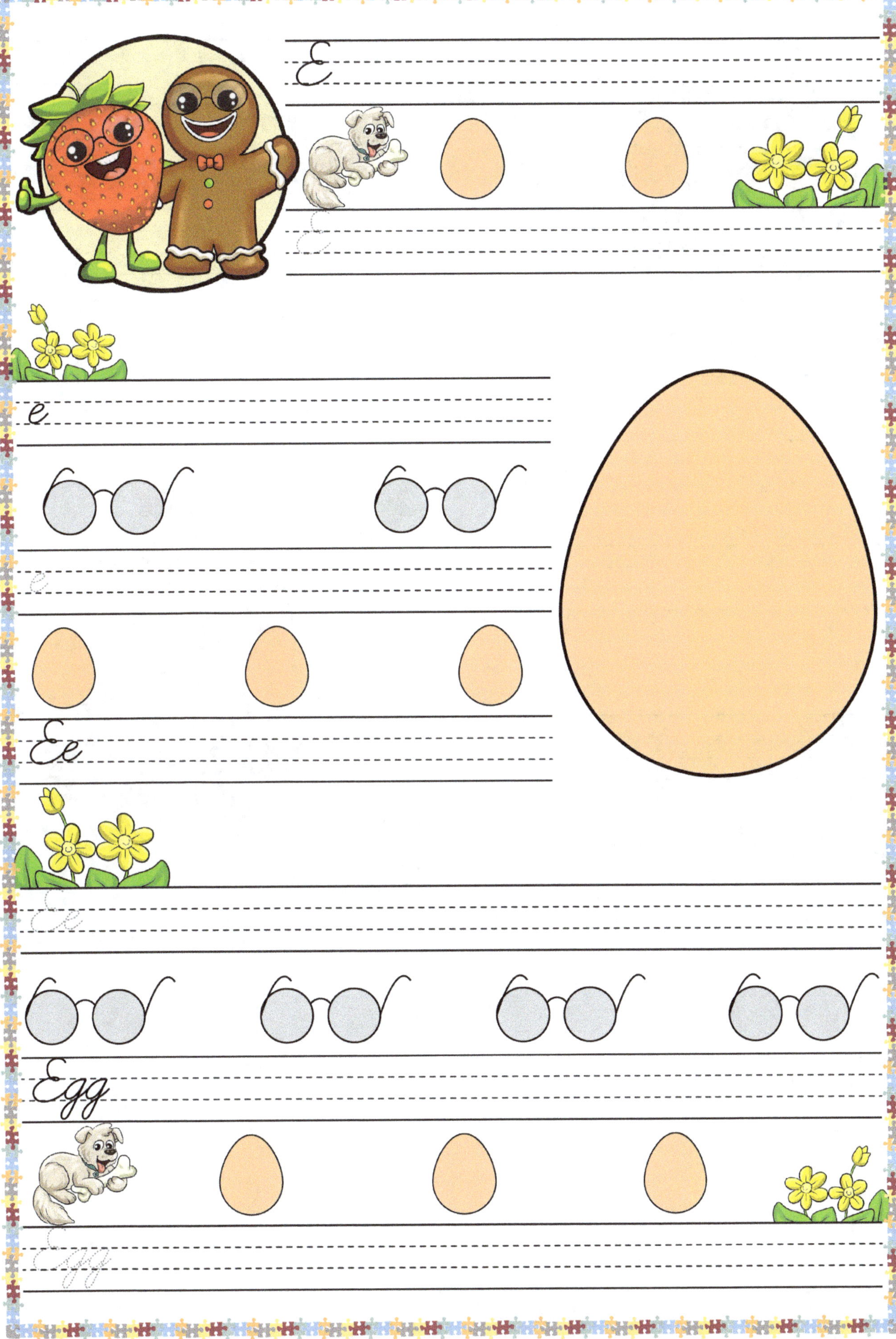
E
e
Ee
Egg

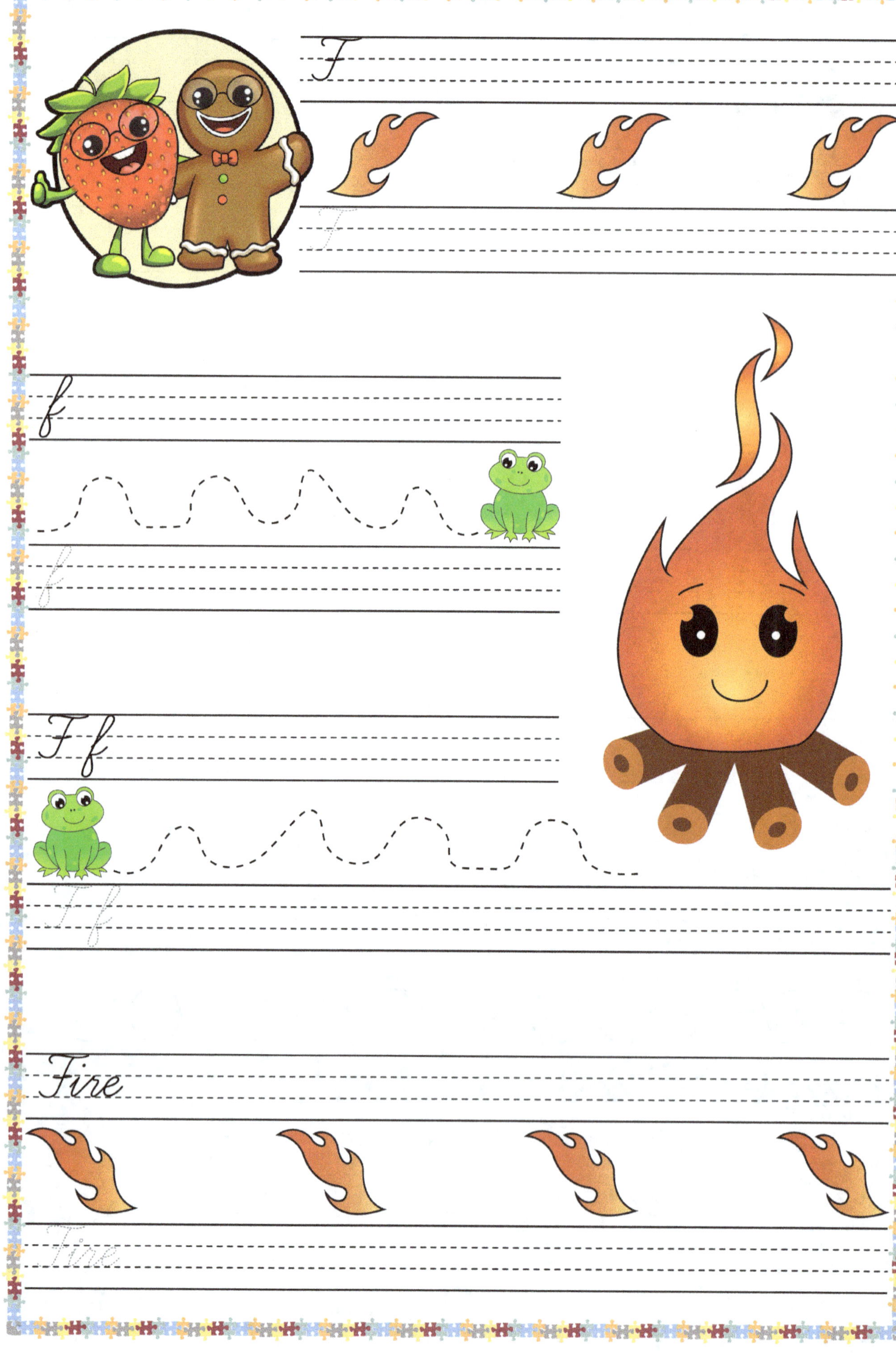

F

f

F f

Fire

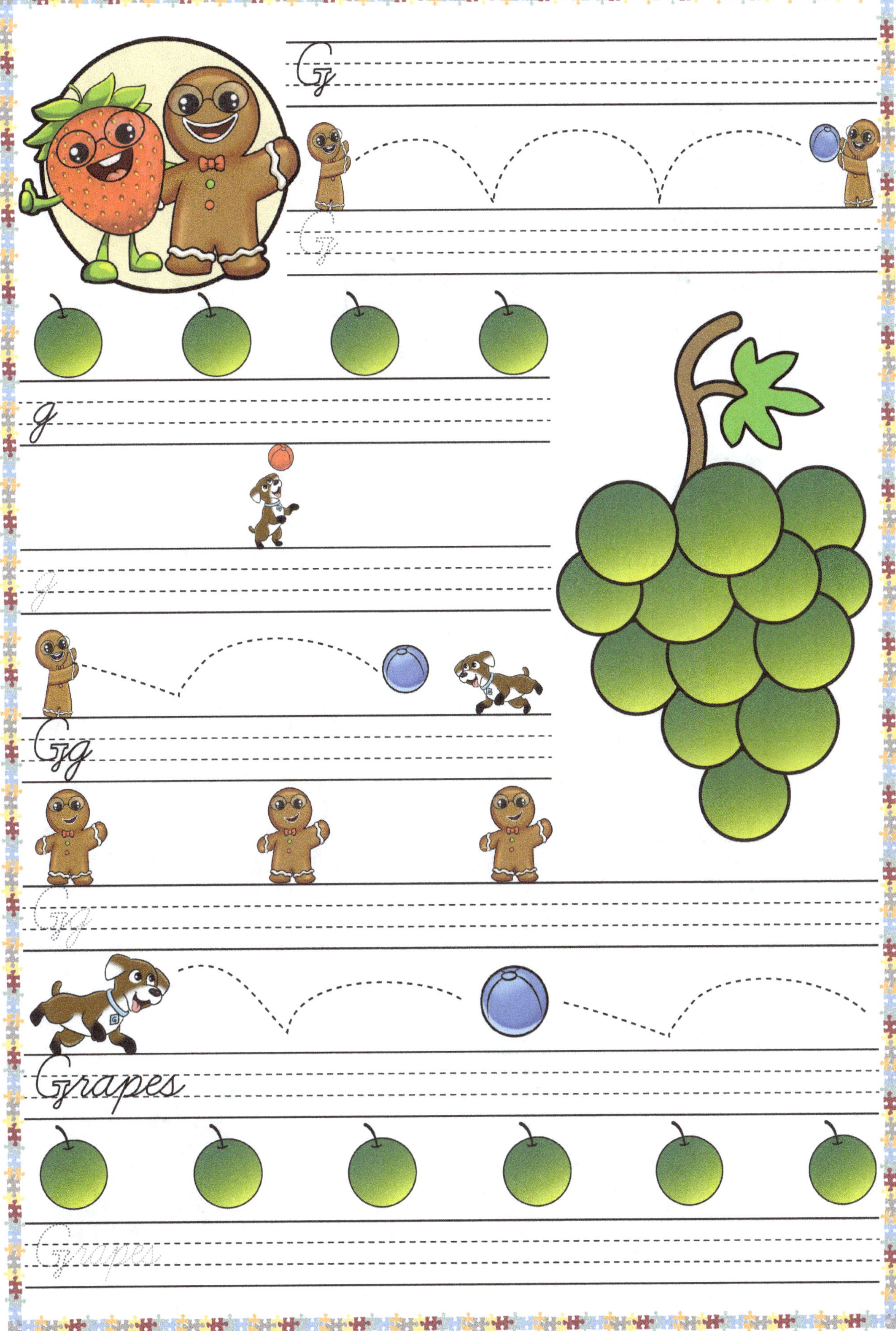
Gg
g
Gg
Grapes

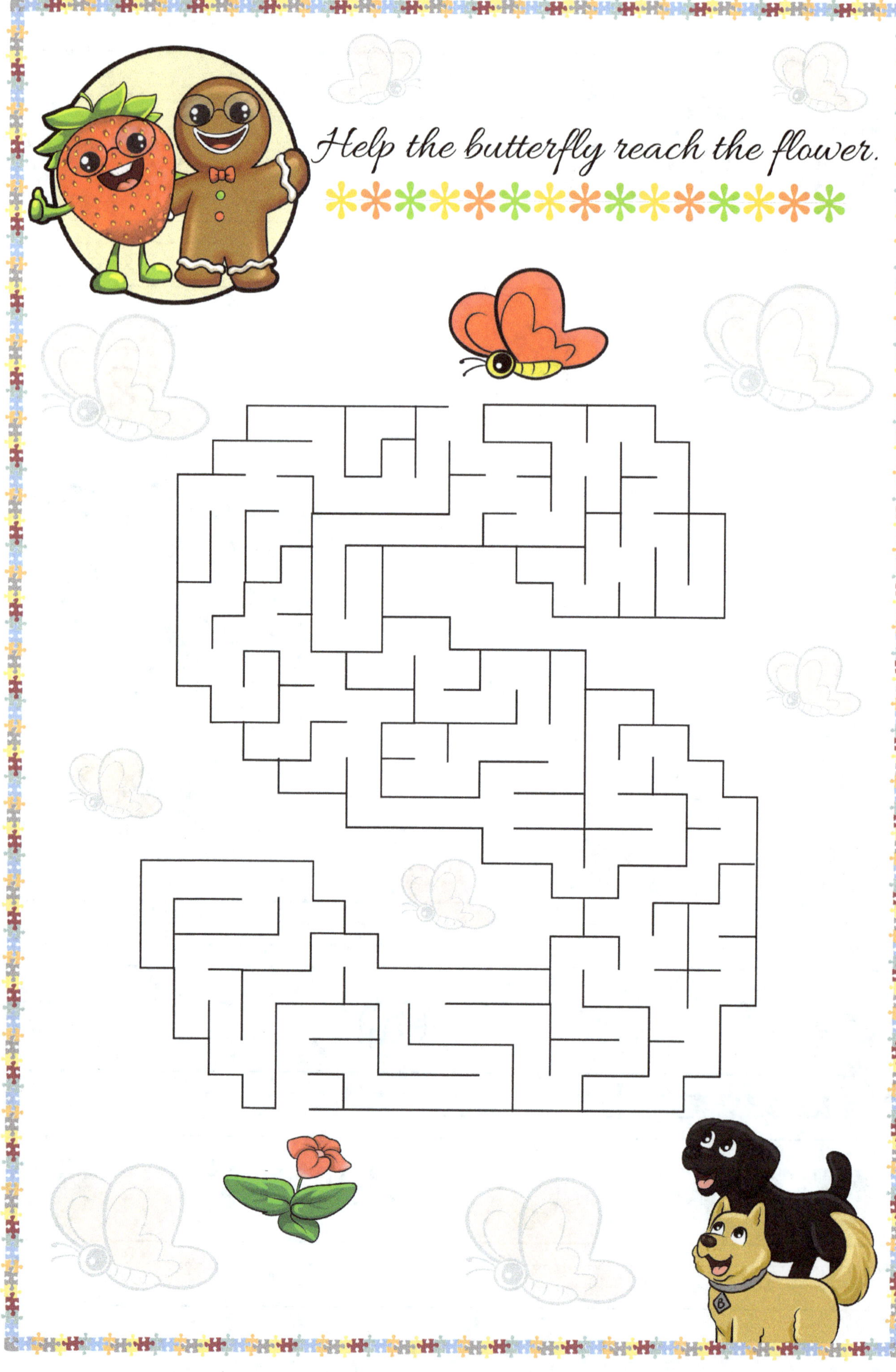

Help the butterfly reach the flower.

Help the butterfly reach the flower.

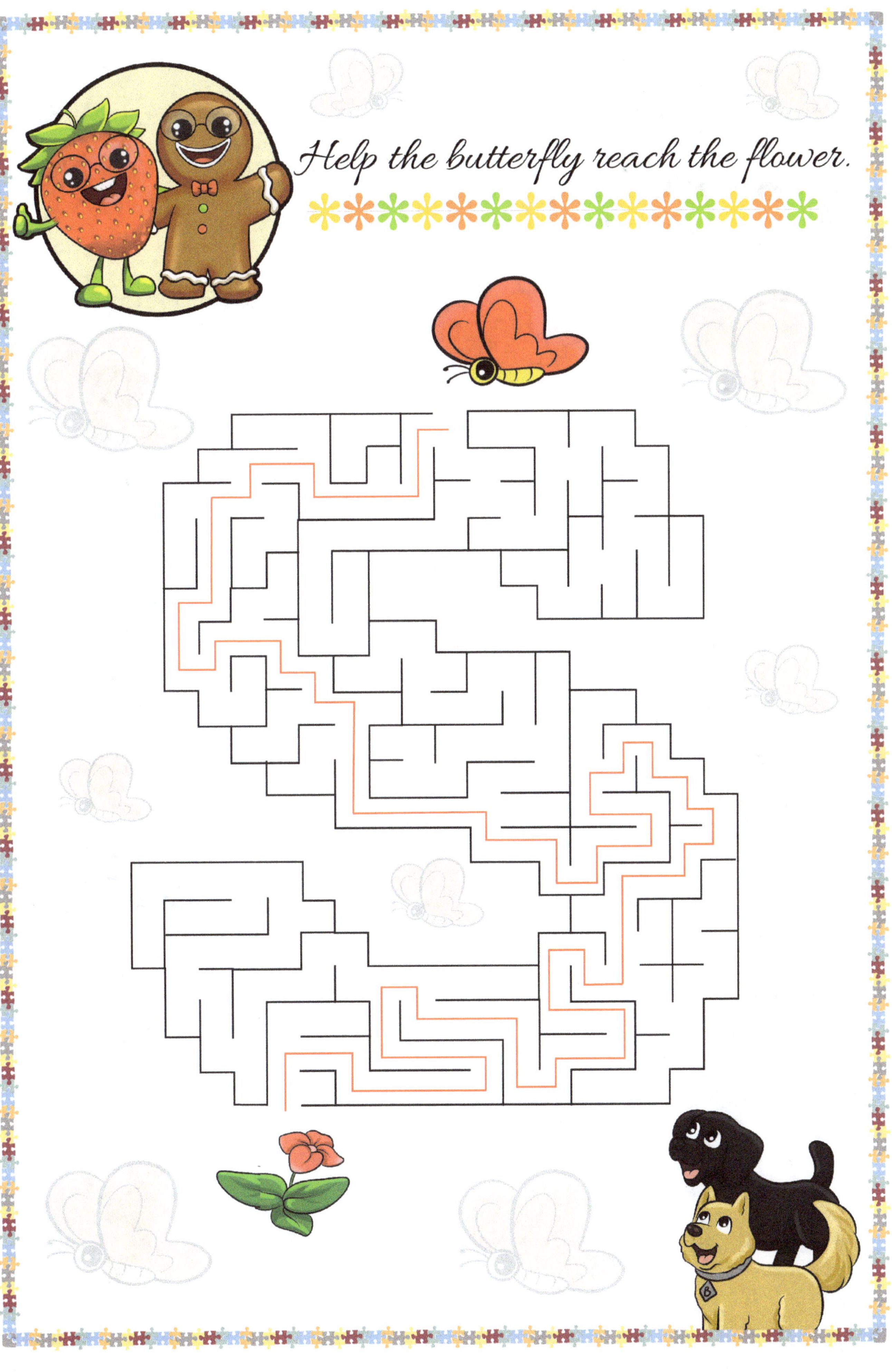

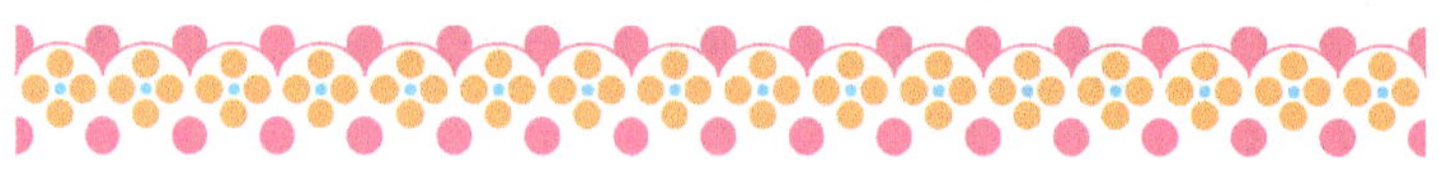
Draw a line to the matching item.

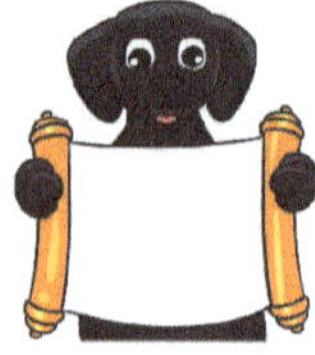

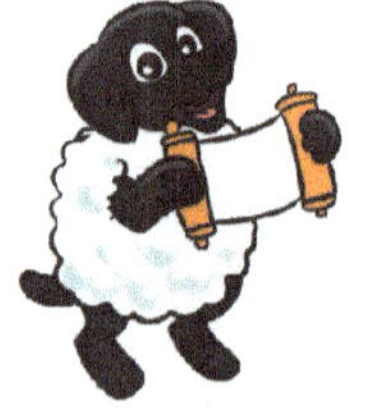

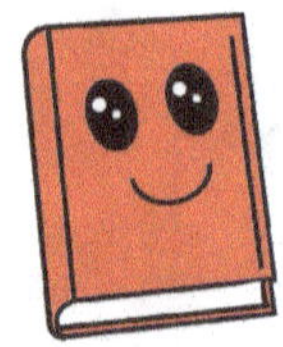

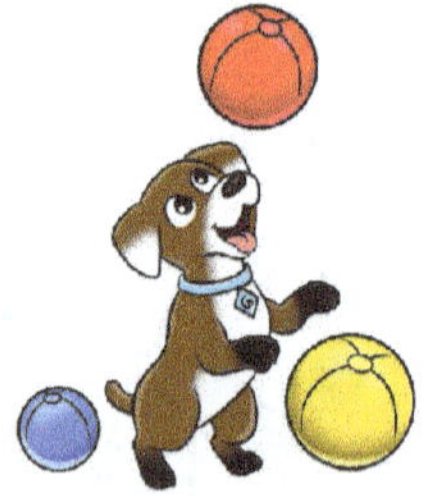

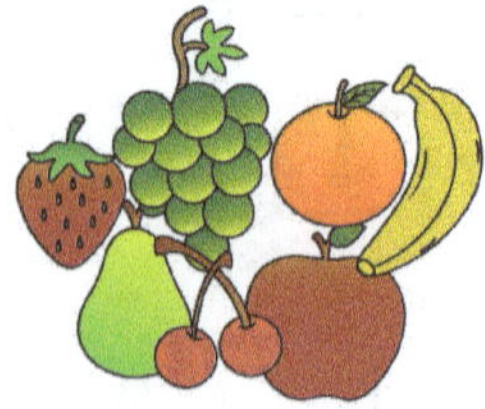

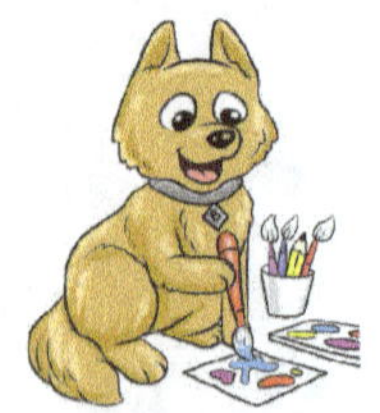

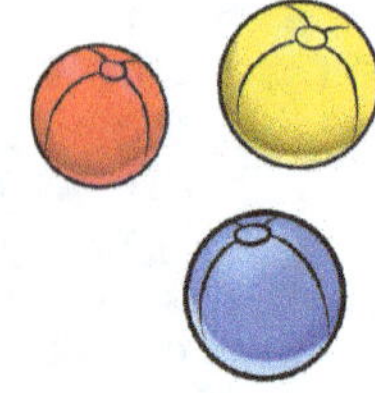

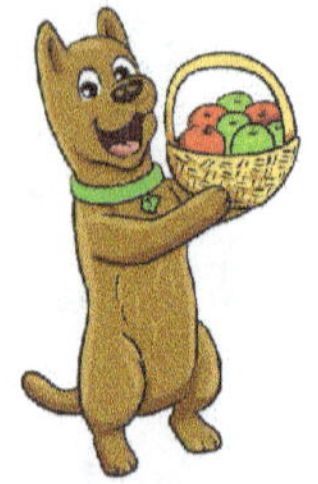

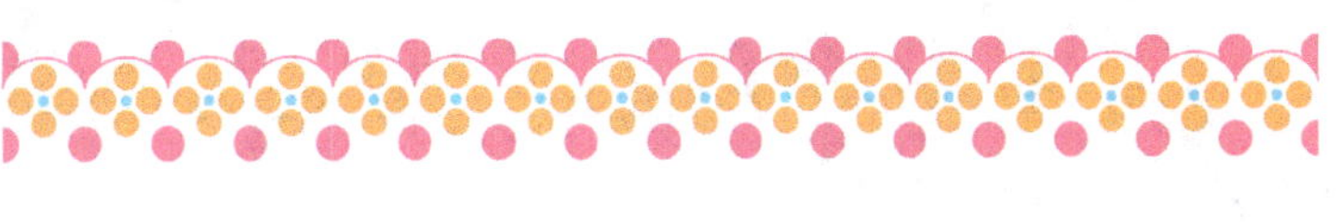

Draw a line to the matching item.

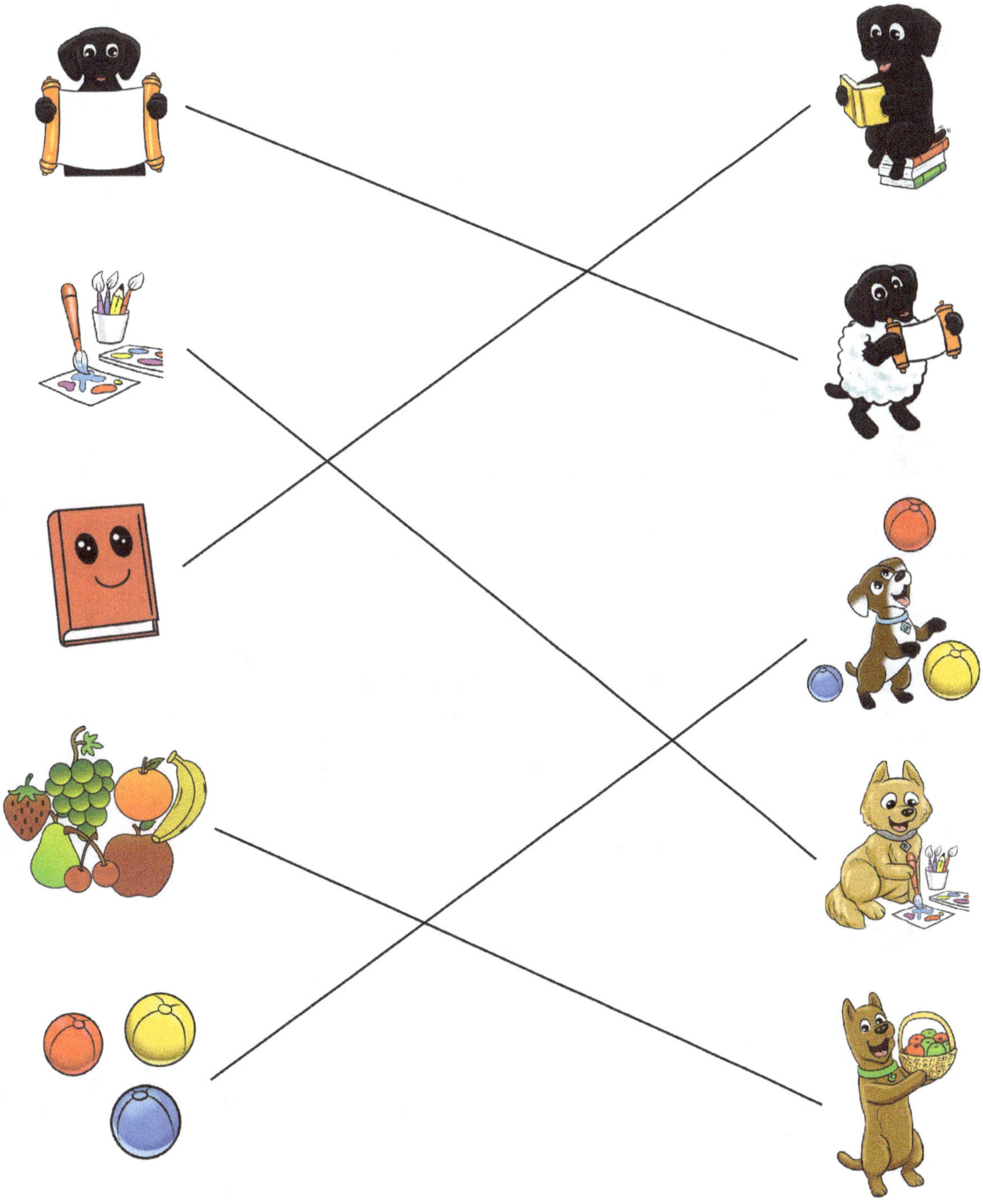

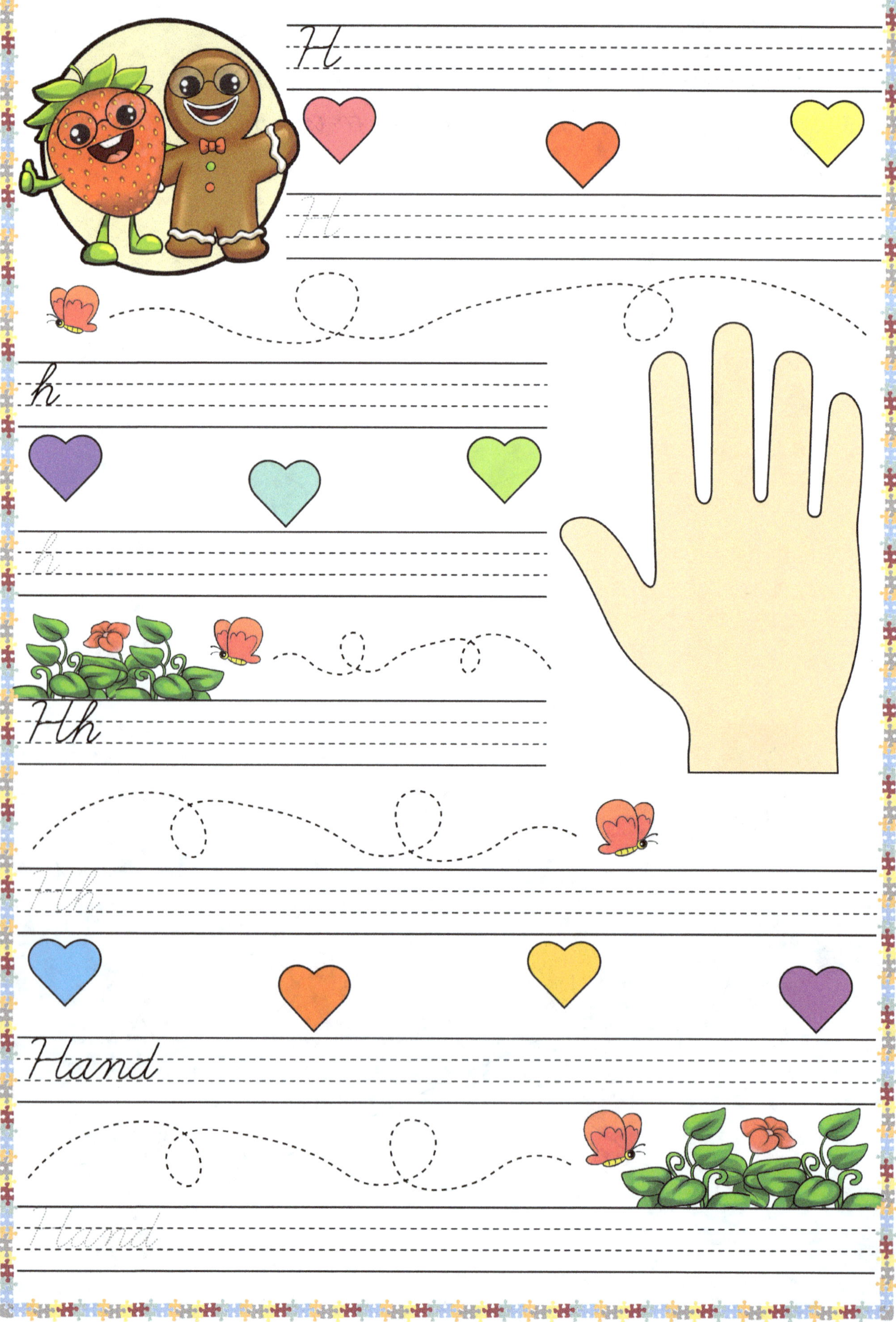

H
H
h
h
Hh
Hh
Hand
Hand

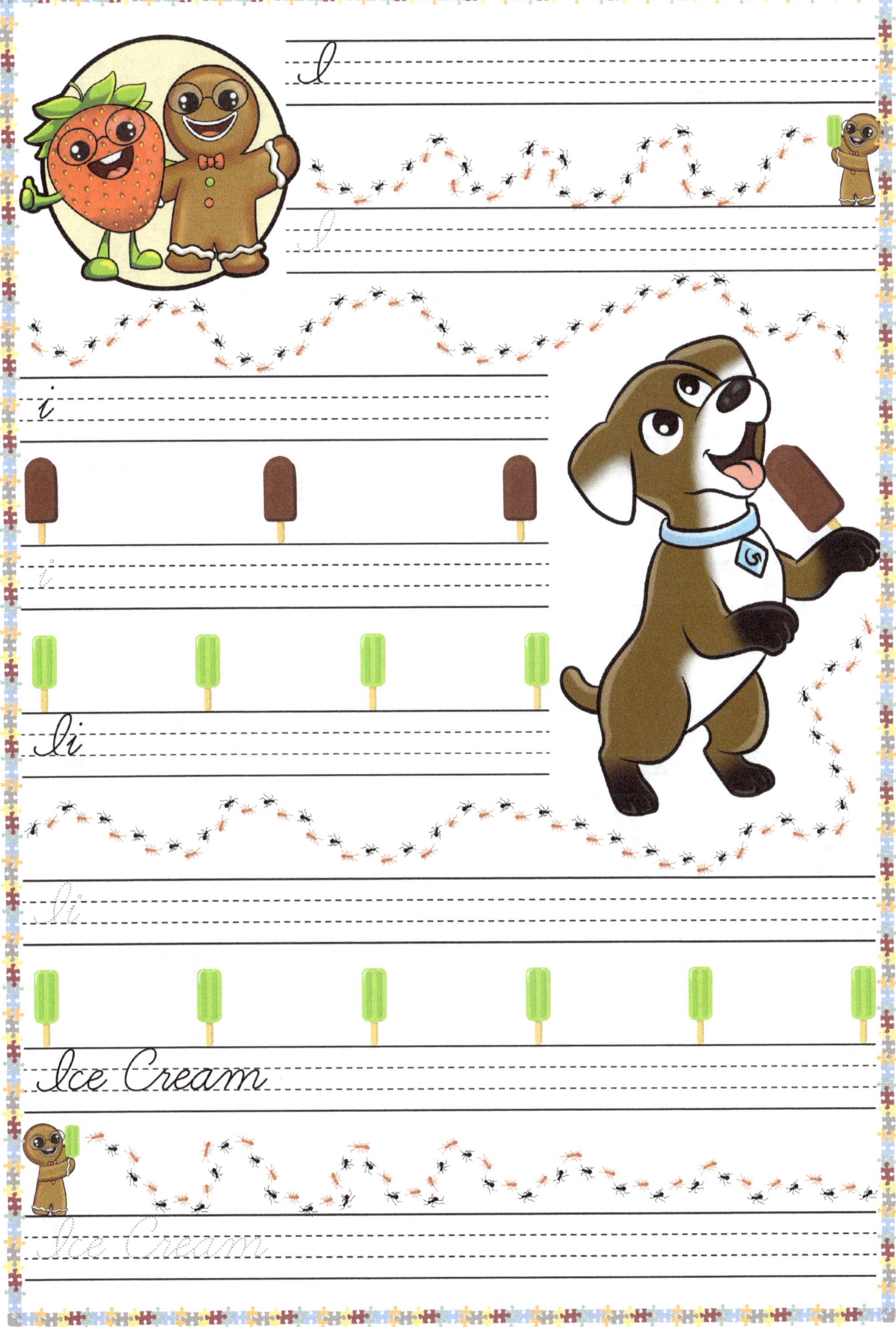

I

i

Ii

Ice Cream

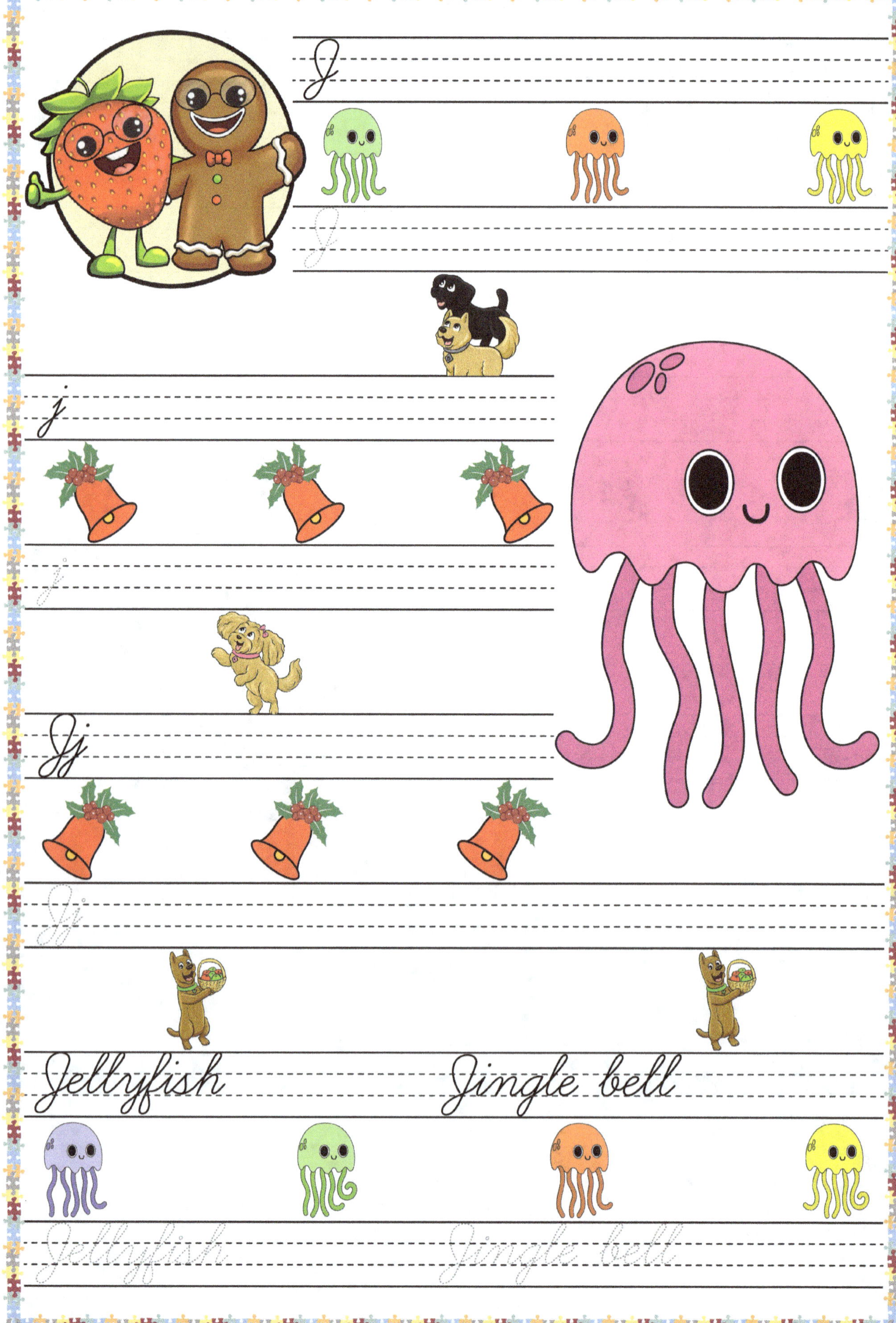

J

j

Jj

Jellyfish

Jingle bell

Jellyfish

Jingle bell

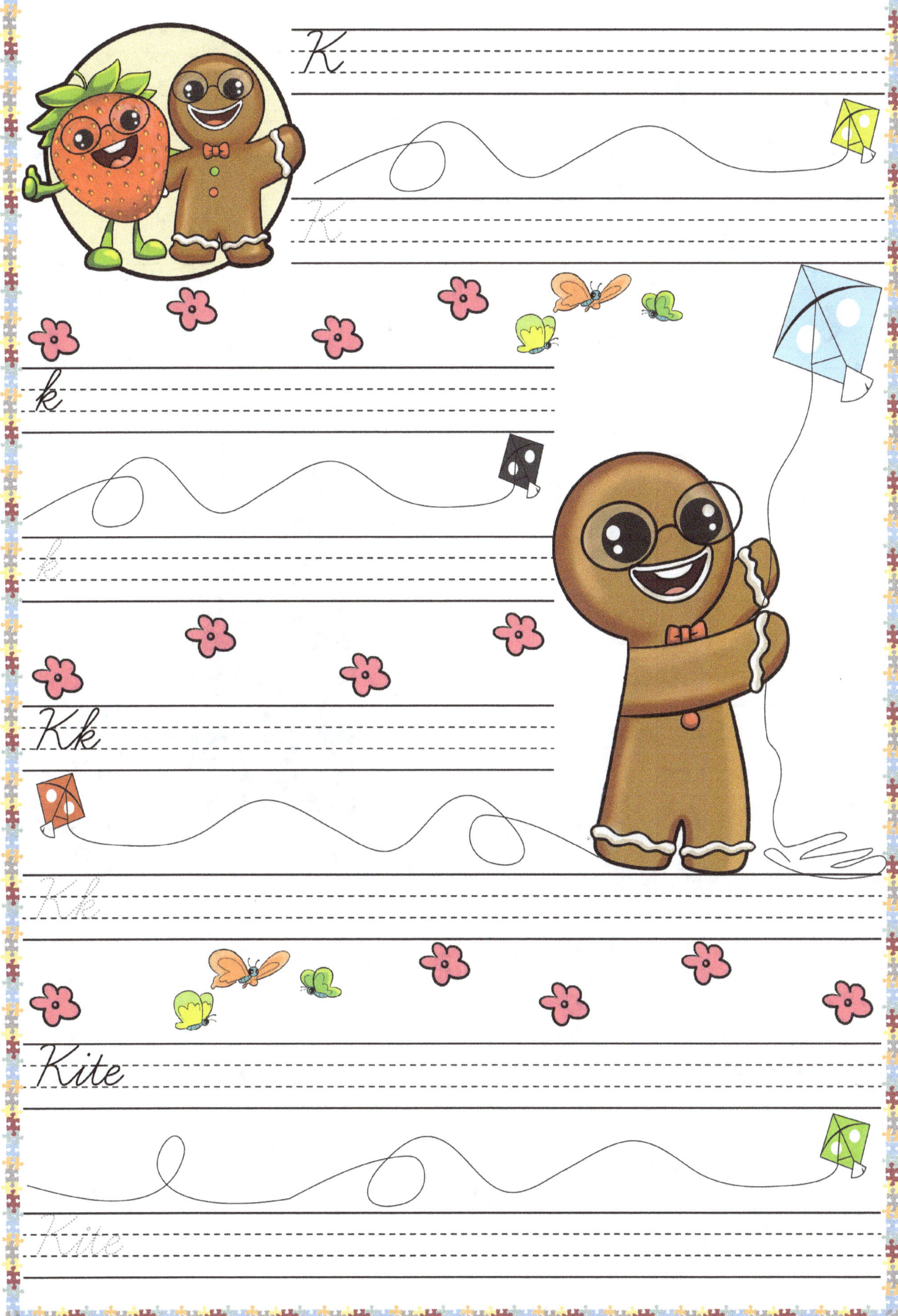

K

K

k

k

Kk

Kk

Kite

Kite

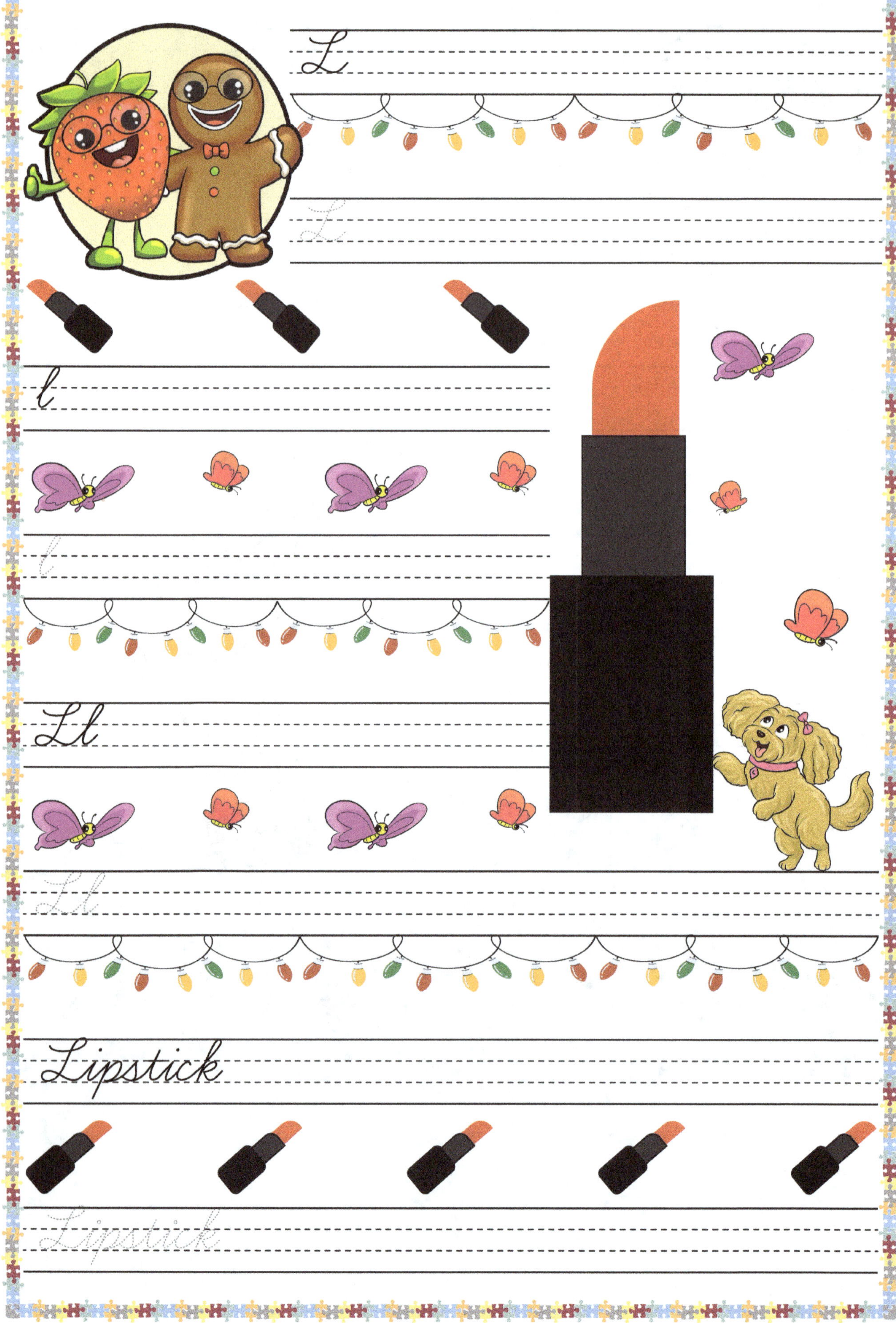

L

L

l

l

Ll

Ll

Lipstick

Lipstick

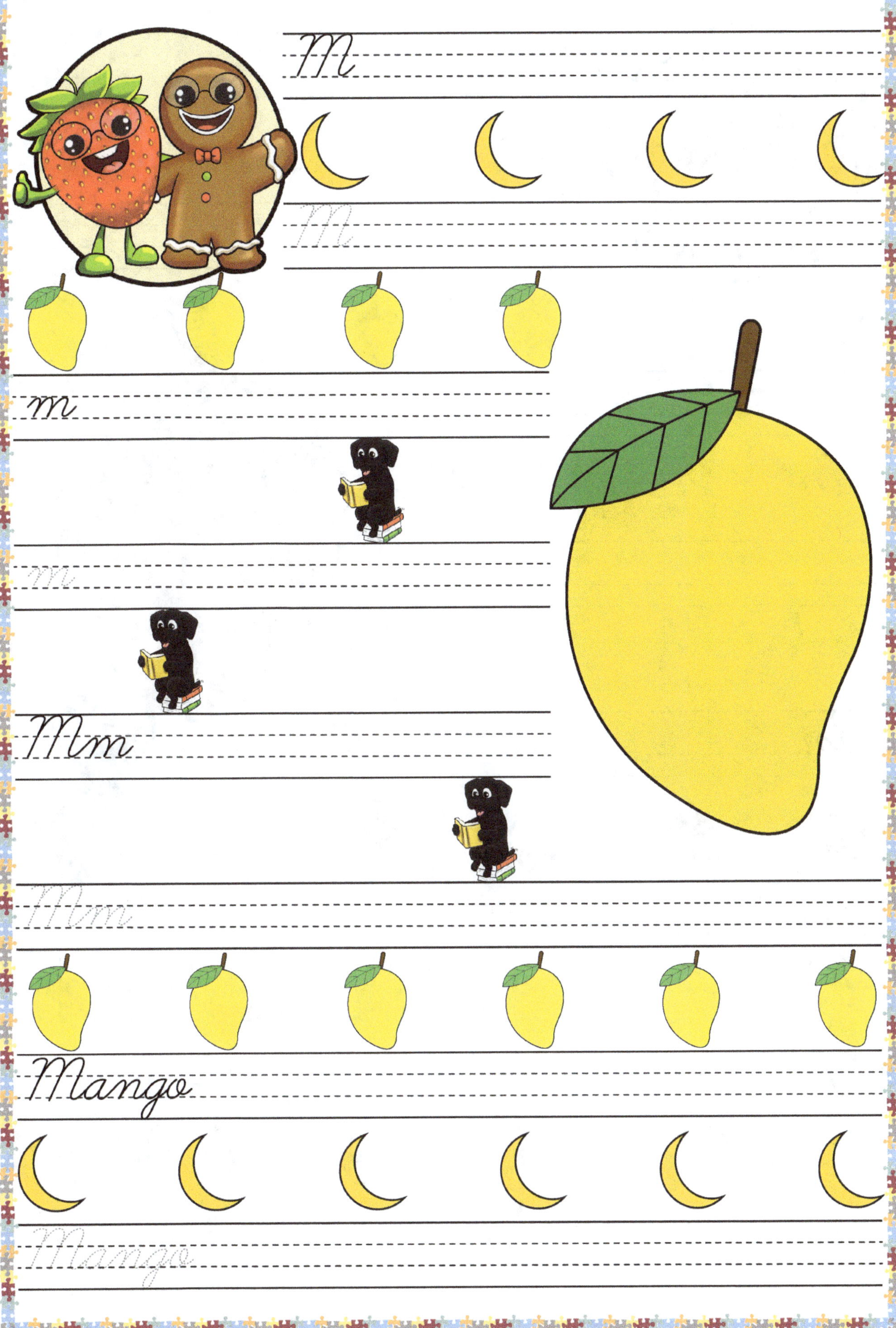

M

m

m

Mm

Mm

Mango

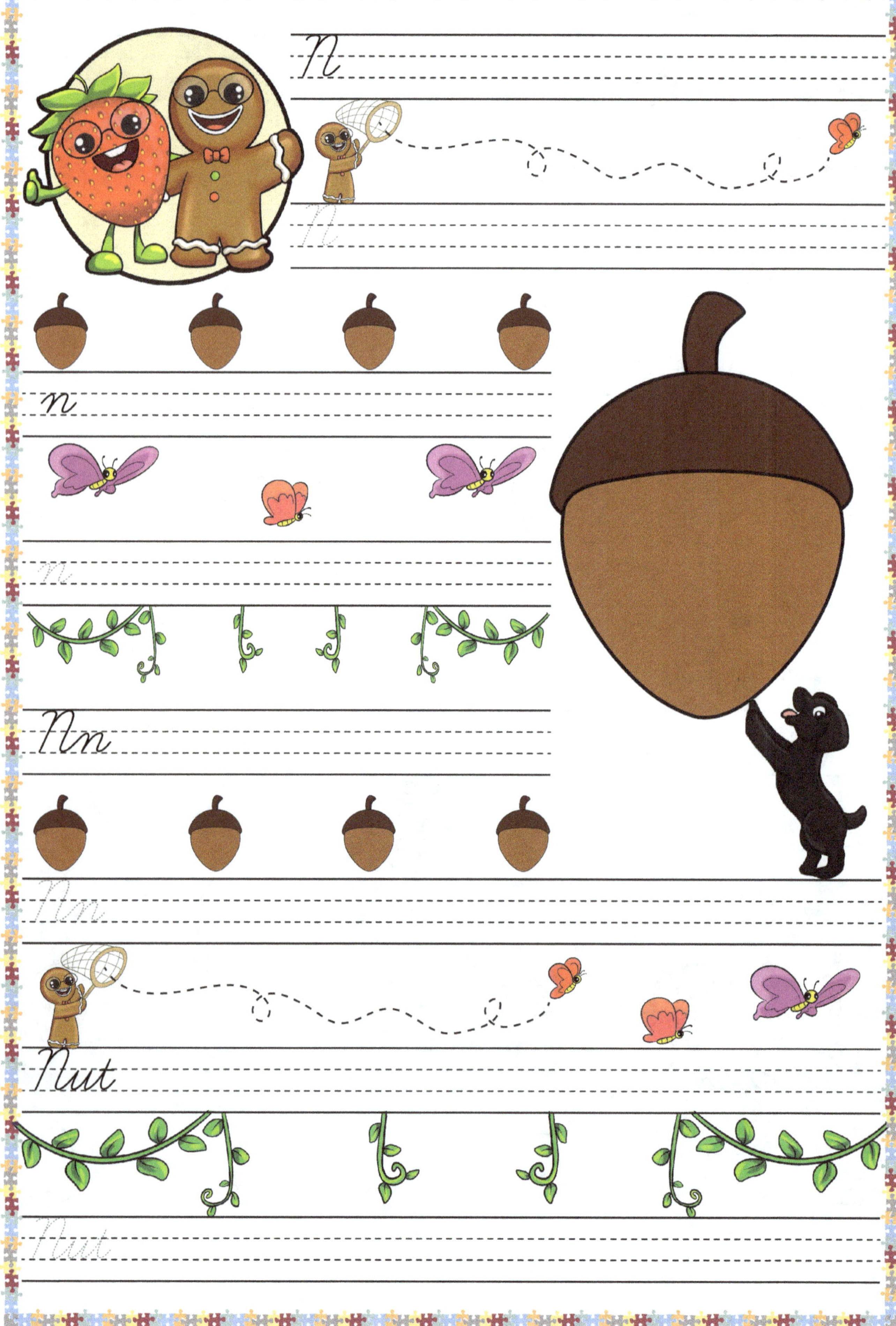

N
N
n
n
Nn
Nn
Nut
Nut

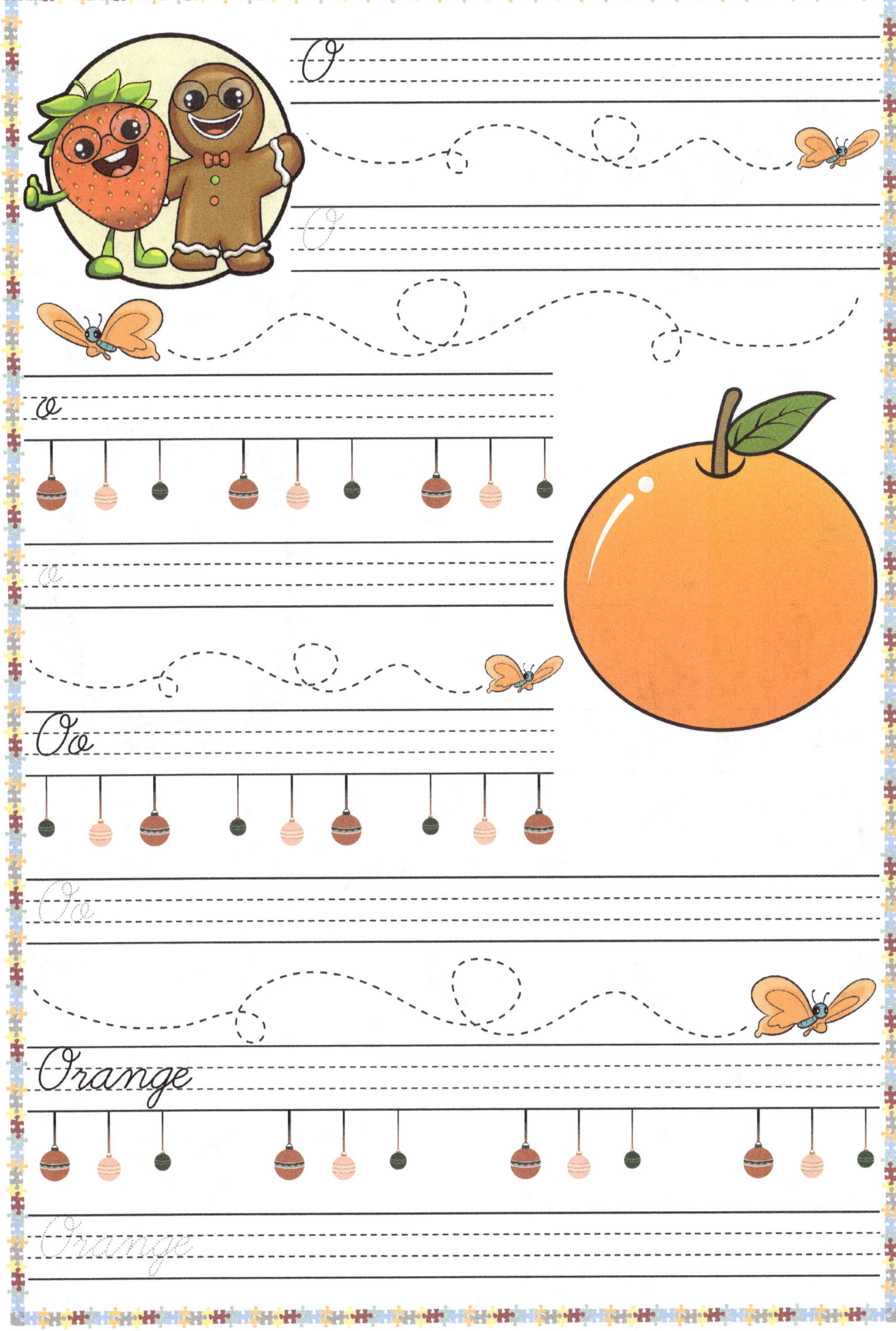

O

O

O

Oo

Oo

Orange

Orange

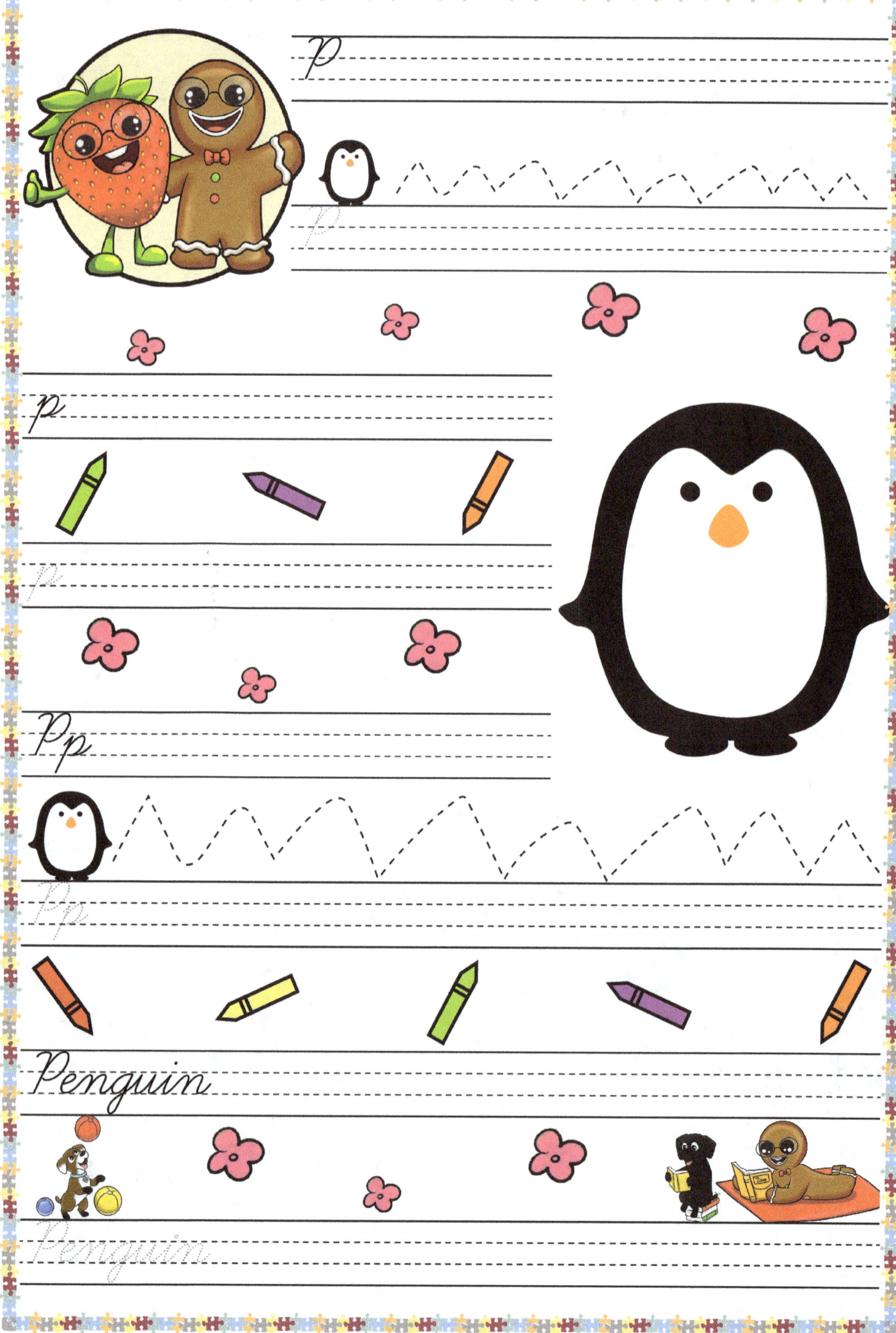

P

P

P

P

Pp

Pp

Penguin

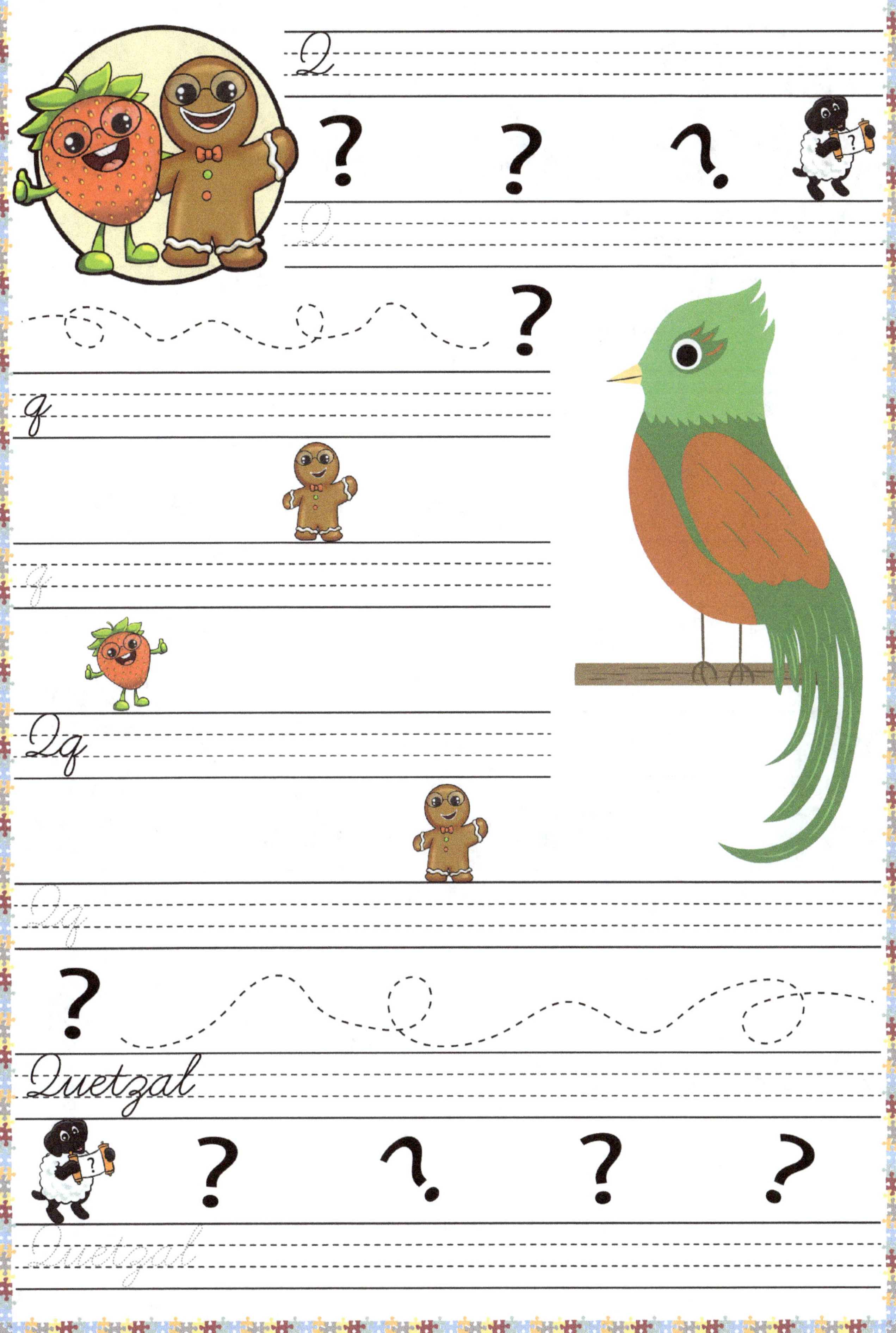

2

q

2q

Quetzal

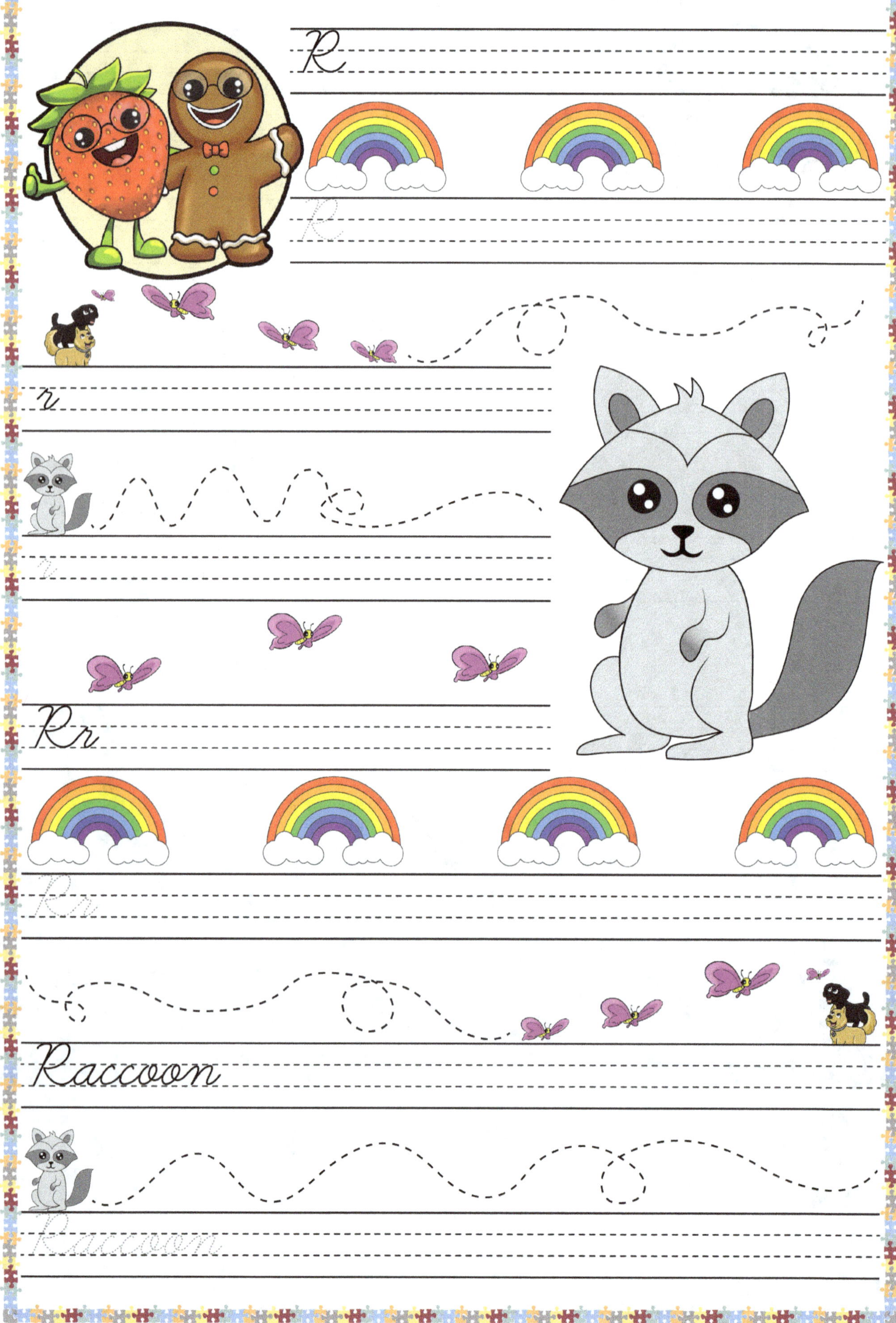

R
R
r
Rr
Raccoon

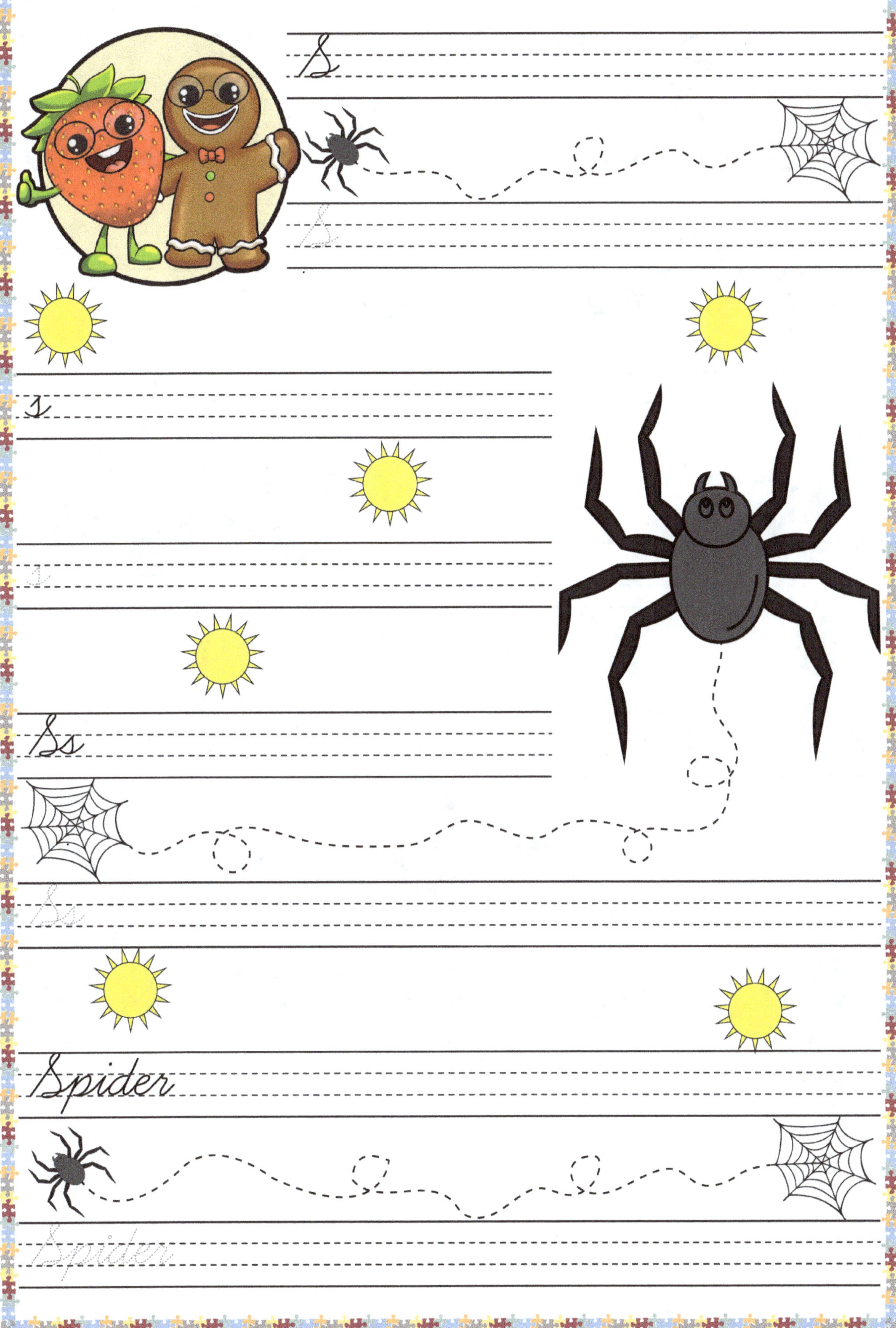

Ss
Ss
Spider
Spider

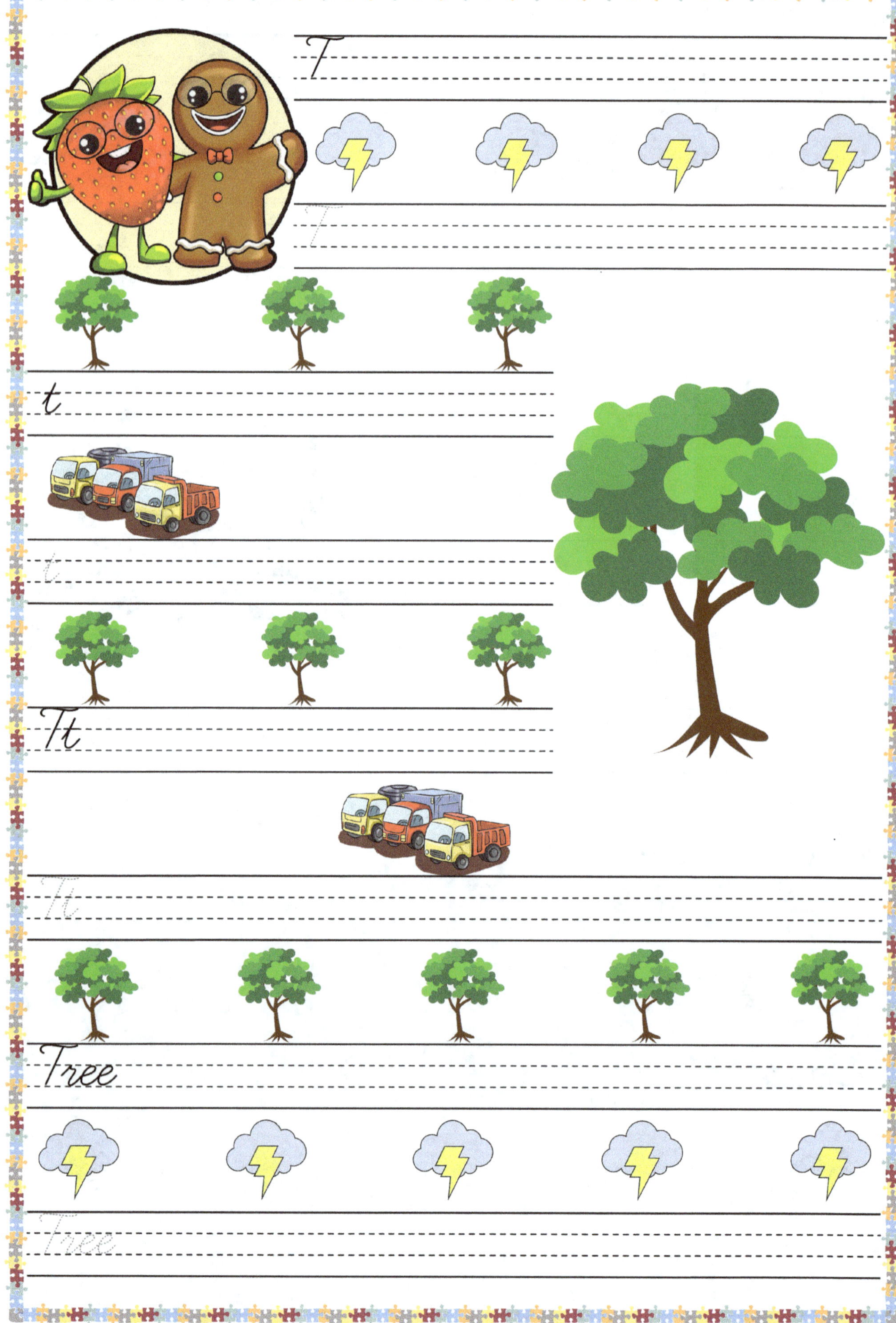
T
t
Tt
Tree

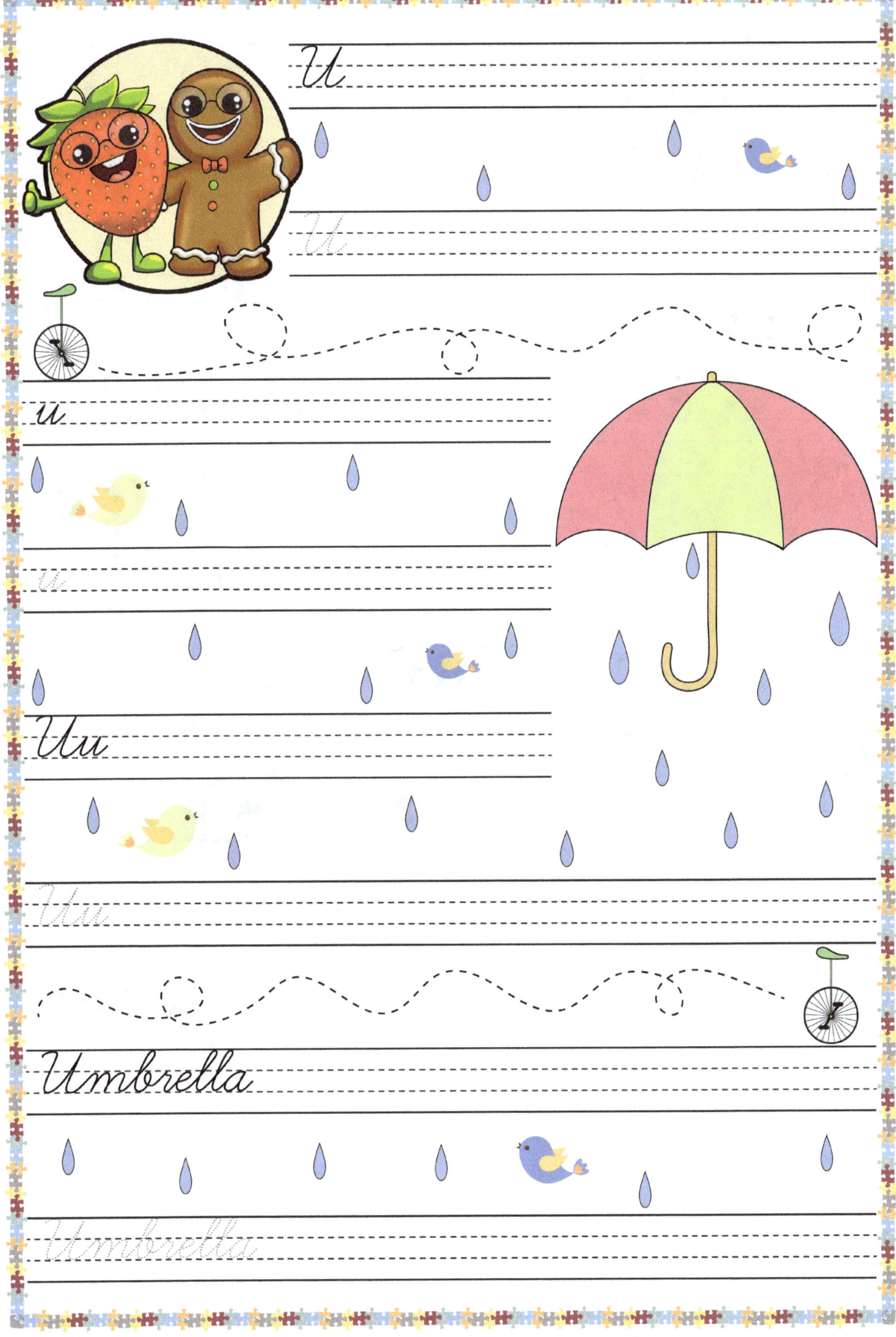

U

u

Uu

Umbrella

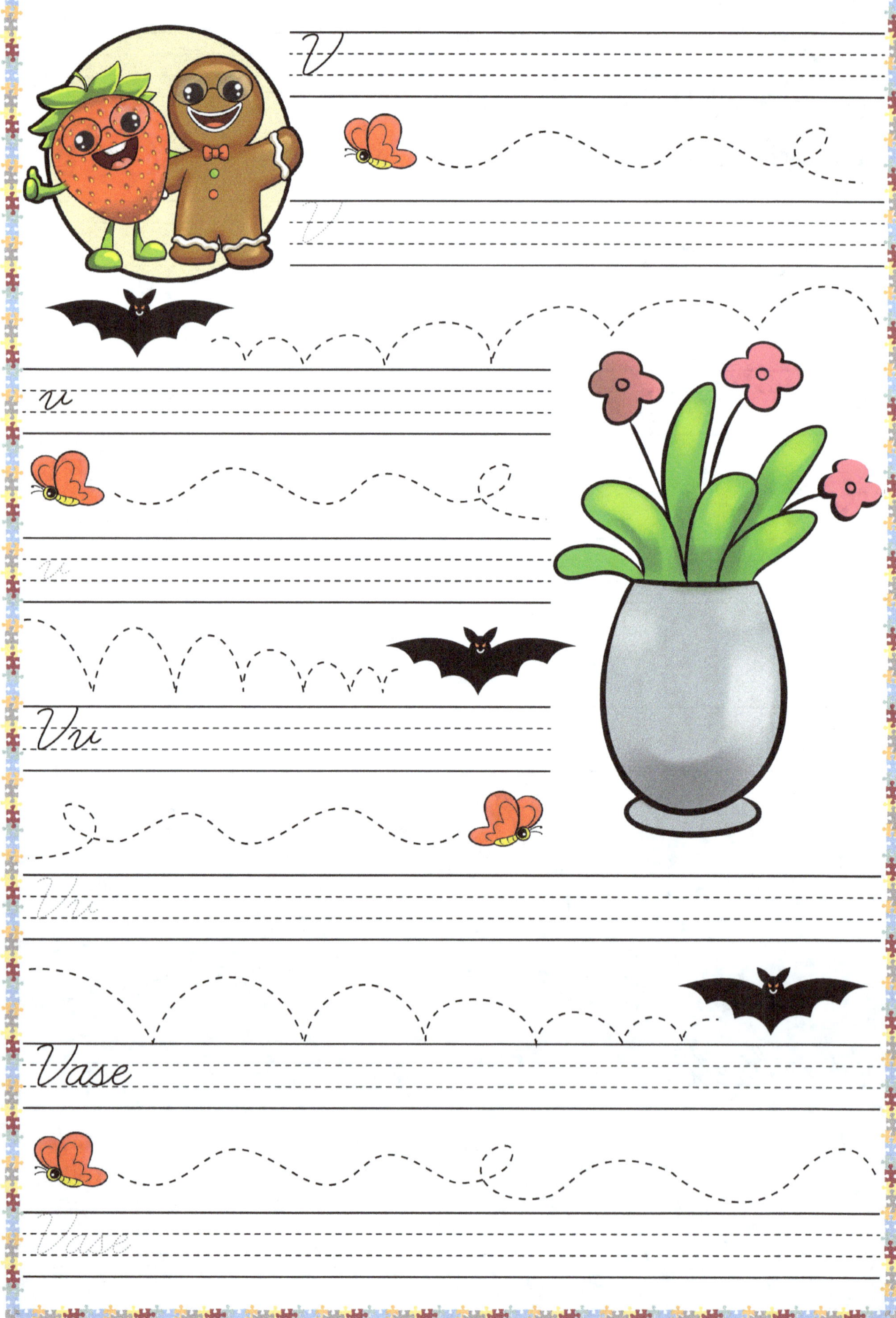
V
V
v
v
Vv
Vv
Vase
Vase

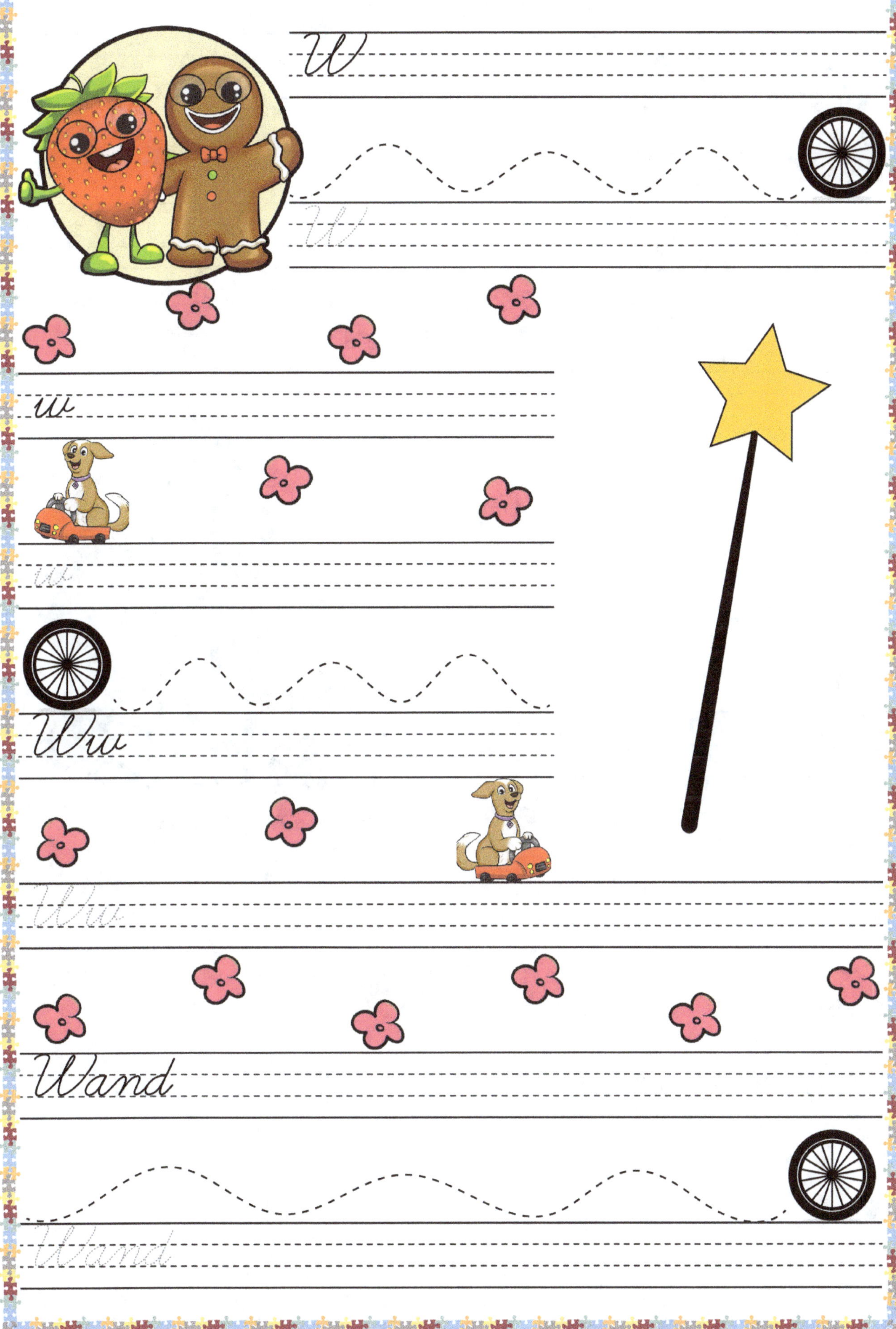

W
W
w
w
Ww
Ww
Wand
Wand

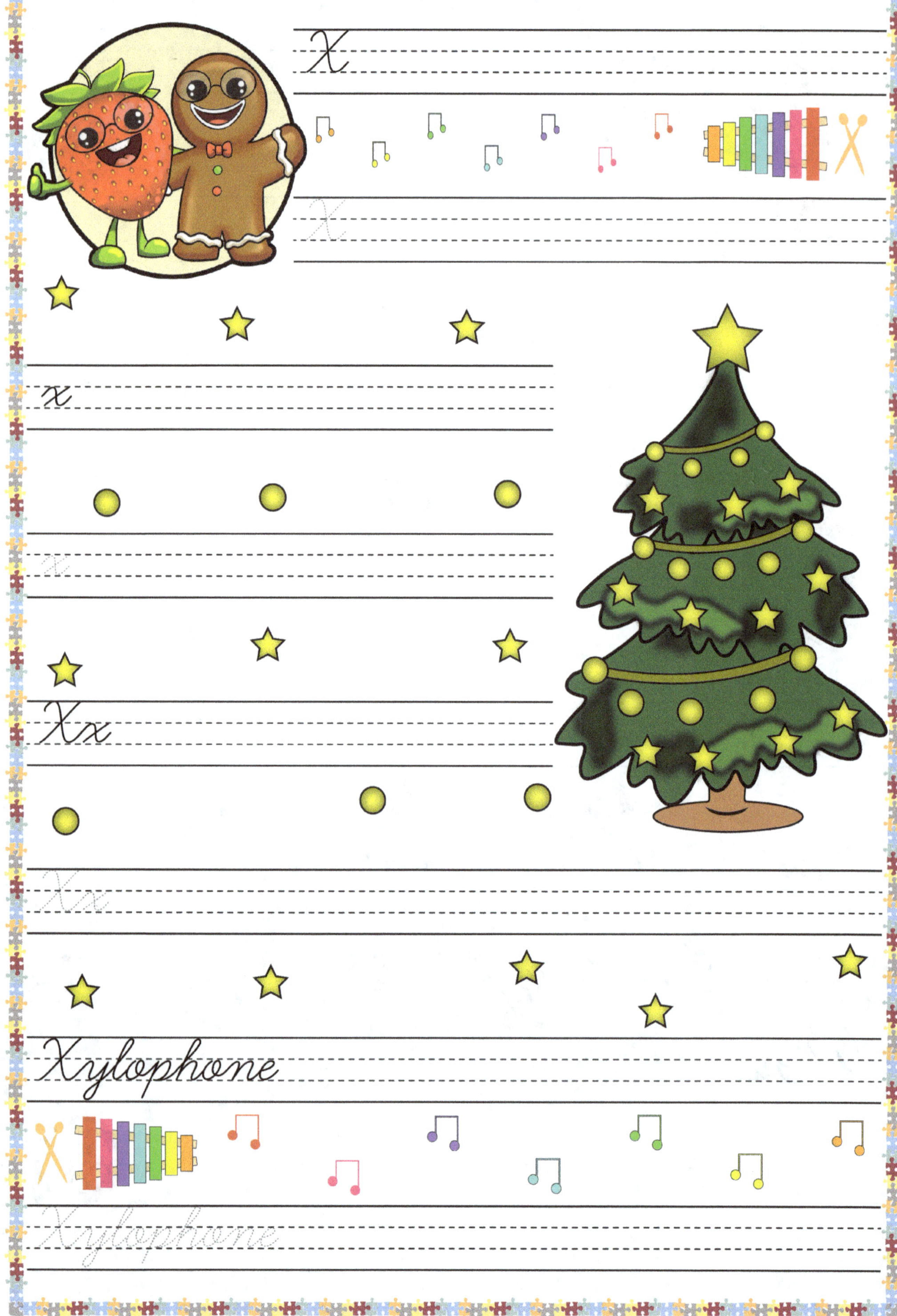

X

x

Xx

Xylophone

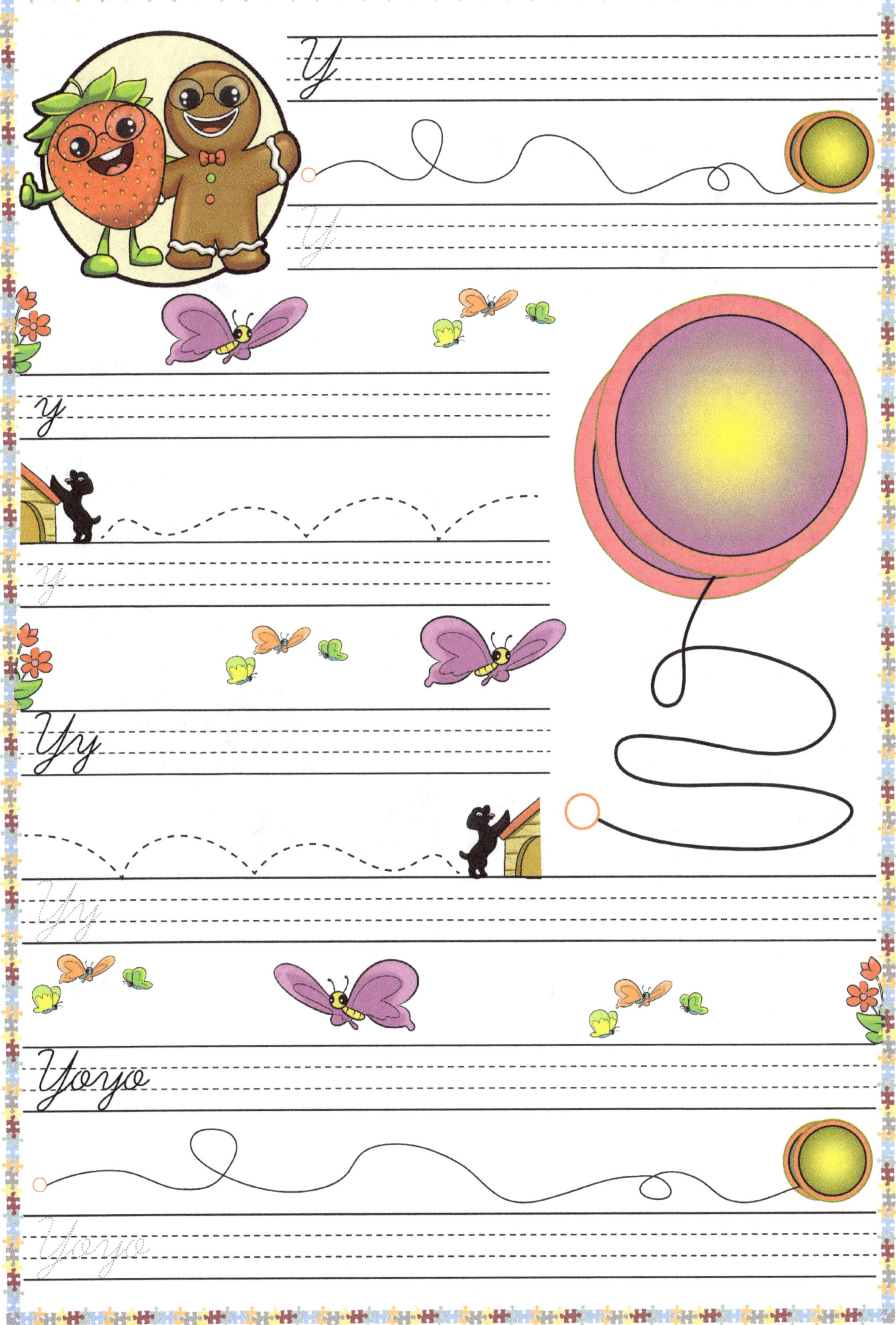

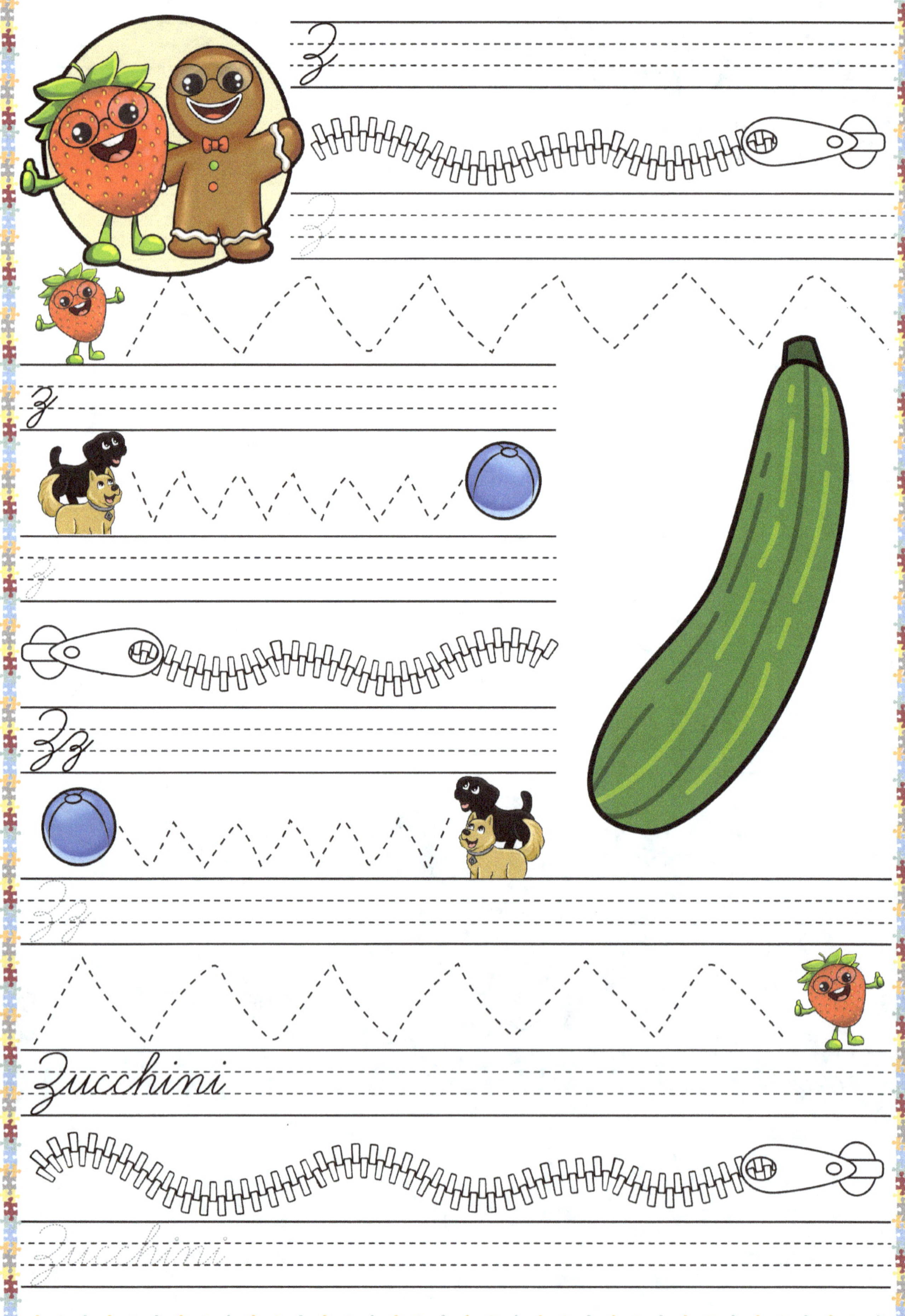

Zucchini

www.ingramcontent.com/pod-product-compliance
Lightning Source LLC
Chambersburg PA
CBHW081242130726
47997CB00009B/2977